Prepared
for
Greatness

RAY BEVAN

PUBLISHED BY RAYLA MINISTRIES

First Published in 2004 by
Rayla Ministries
69 Lower Dock Street, Newport, South Wales NP20 1EH, UK

ISBN 0-9546941-0-4

Designed by Xheight Limited
Back Cover Portrait by Ellis Photography
Printed by Bell & Bain Limited

ACKNOWLEDGEMENTS

First of all I want to thank the Holy Spirit without whom I would have nothing to write about.

Of course, my wife Laila, for her positive encouragement and persistent exhortation to get the book finished.

To my office staff for deciphering sometimes unintelligent writing and getting it to print.

To my friends who have given their endorsements adding credibility to the content.

To Carol Thomas for her generous sacrifice of time to layout and design this book.

Thank you also to Alan Jefferies for his help in punctuation and grammar.

ENDORSEMENTS

I met Ray Bevan when I first became a Christian many years ago. I saw this guy who looked like an out of work rocker instead of a pastor. He was full of joy and bubbling with life. His love for God just shone out of him. I knew that I wanted my Christian life to be like this. From that first meeting we have remained friends and he has helped me to grow tremendously in my Christian life. Ray is a true man of God and has been blessed through his obedience to the Lord.

This book is a great help to Christians and non-Christians because it deals with real issues. It is written in a way that is easy to understand yet very thought provoking. It is a must for any bookshelf. It will help people to grow and will make people look at Jesus in a different way.

Bobby Ball

My friend Ray Bevan is a rare gift of communication. Complex truth presented by him is understood and appreciated by everybody. *"Prepared for Greatness"* is a case in point. This book will level the road for untold readers who wish to arrive right there. I recommend it highly.

Reinhard Bonnke, Evangelist

Rich insights on God's grace and how to live in his presence each day. I thoroughly enjoyed it – you will too!

Bob Gass, Author - The World For You Today

Ray's great sense of humour comes through the way he communicates profound truths and in this book, he shares some hilarious personal anecdotes to illustrate the ways God prepares us for His purpose for our lives.

Brian Houston, Senior Pastor, Hillsong Church, Australia

I must confess, I'm a little jealous. What a special gift, God has given to Ray Bevan – What conscience piercing insight – What self-depicting humour – What a Godly grace to exhort and encourage.

This book is for people like me, who have felt disappointed, mistake ridden and disqualified. It will inspire those who have blown it, to strengthen their grip on God's grace. To dare to believe that God *will* use them, in spite of their public humiliation.

It is a must read for everyone who assumes they are not a Pharisee – like me. It's time to take off our masks.

Terry Law

He's a bundle of dynamic energy behind the pulpit and a preacher who could have become a stand-up comedian. He's had me rolling on the floor with his numerous hilarious stories, many of them gleaned from personal experiences.

But Ray Bevan is not just a good storyteller. No, he has a burning message in his heart of the love and mercy of the Lord Jesus Christ.

His book, *Prepared for Greatness*, is about recognising the Divine Hand of God in one's life. As Ray says in his introduction, "You are not an accident' and that is something that so many Christians, including church leaders, need to know these days.

It seems that when some Christians hit a brick wall they lose all hope and faith of God who has said He will always be there for His children.

Ray's book emphasises that God has a plan and a purpose for all of us and when that is firmly imbedded in our hearts we will not falter when the going gets hard.

This is an inspiring book and Ray shares some of the dark moments in his life and the great spiritual lessons he has learned from them.

Pastor Ray McCauley, Rhema Ministries, South Africa

Ray Bevan brings a wonderful blend of practical encouragement and Biblical insight in the book '*Prepared for Greatness*' I was empowered as I ready about the sovereignty with which God brought me into this world. You and I are not coincidences or accidents but wonderful works of God.

Pastor Bevan will help you be prepared and positioned for the destiny the Lord has for you. You, like me, will be encouraged and empowered to your next level in life.

Casey Treat, Sr. Pastor, Christian Faith Centre, USA

CONTENTS

INTRODUCTION

You Are Not An Accident!

I have heard many preachers say many things, but one thing in particular has had a profound effect upon my life. It was simply that we are the result of three things: sovereignty, predestination and purpose. We are not the result of sex, but of sovereignty. Before you were a seed in your father's loins, you were a seed in the heart of God. Before you were formed in your mother's womb, you were formed in the mind of God. The sex that brought you into the world may have been illegitimate, but you are not. You were known by the sovereignty of God and he chose you to be born here, on planet Earth. It's amazing that out of millions of sperm, you were one little tadpole fighting for the prize. Only one sperm would have the amazing privilege of penetrating the egg that was being formed ready for life on earth – and that tadpole was you!

Don't ever say that you are an accident. Don't ever feel stigmatised and inferior because of the way you entered this world. Your arrival on planet Earth was not an accident; it was planned in God's sovereignty. What God said to Jeremiah, I believe he says to us all – *'Before I formed you in the womb I knew you; before you were born I sanctified you; I ordained you a prophet to the nations' (Jer. 1:5)*. You are not a result of your parents, but of predestination. David wrote, *'Your eyes saw my substance, being yet unformed. And in Your book they were all written, the days fashioned for me, when as yet there were none of them' (Ps. 139:16)*.

Many people look at their background, their upbringing, the colour of their skin, the family they were born into, their lack of education or their past circle of friends and say to themselves, 'If I had been given a better start in life my destiny in God would be much more effective.'

Perhaps you feel you were never wanted as a child, perhaps you were made to feel useless; perhaps all your life you have lived with a crippling sense of inadequacy – the result of negative words being continually spoken into your life, or maybe of deplorable acts done against your person. It could also be that your childhood was a happy one, that you were raised in a Christian home and surrounded by love, protection and godly parents. To others it would be an upbringing to be envied, but to you it seems a disadvantage. You feel you've been too sheltered, wrapped up in cotton wool and shielded from the real world.

I recently heard a preacher say that he sometimes wished he had been a drug addict, a pimp or a gangster, so that when he got saved his gratitude and love for Jesus would have been greater. He was thinking of the prostitute who had been forgiven by Jesus, and outwardly and openly showed her gratitude and love before a religious crowd, washing Jesus' feet with her tears and wiping them with her hair. Jesus turned to the religious crowd, who were appalled at such a show of affection and at the fact that Jesus should receive it from such a woman, and said, *'She loves much because she has been forgiven much.'*

You may feel like that preacher. What testimonies have I got? Compared to others, what have I got that can contribute to changing this world? I'm just so ordinary, so predictable, so boring. If I had had a different start in life my influence would be so much more effective and powerful.

As I look back over my life, I can see that one of the most important lessons I have learned is that I am special, I am important; I am a unique individual with a unique destiny to discover. I am not an accident, I am not the result of sex or of people – they were just the means to get me here. My real sense of value comes from the knowledge that God knew me before I was even in my mother's womb, and my days were written for me; waiting for me to live them, even before that. The purpose of this book is to encourage you to realise that you were uniquely created, and even at this moment you are being uniquely prepared for the next season of your life.

As I think about my own upbringing in the light of how God is using me now, I laugh at how God took my early years, even before I knew him, and weaved them into the fabric of my destiny. You don't need to waste your time wishing you'd had a better, or different, start in life. You are not an accident: what you see as useless, unattractive and unspectacular, God sees as potential to be released and channelled. If God has sovereignly predestined you to be here, there must be a reason and a purpose, for God creates nothing without a purpose or reason. That reason or purpose is your destiny, your calling – it's waiting to be discovered, enjoyed and released.

I read a story of an old sculptor who was passing a friend's farm. He noticed a gnarled tree stump lying on the ground. Shouting to his friend, he asked if he had any need of it. 'Oh no,' replied his friend. 'I'm clearing my garden of all the old rubbish. Why? Do you want it?' 'Yes,' replied the sculptor, who carefully lifted the stump onto his shoulders and carried it to his workshop. He placed it in the centre of the room and paced around it, his eyes dancing with delight, as he spied something inside that old piece of wood that was of great value. Finally, he started to work on the wood, cutting with great passion and deliberation, as if he was trying to free something that was trapped inside. All through the night he worked, and as the early morning sunlight streamed through the window into the room, the old, gnarled, unwanted piece of wood was nowhere to be seen. In its place stood a beautiful sculpted eagle. The old man placed the eagle with pride outside his house. The following day the farmer from whom he had got the old stump passed and commented on the beautiful sculpture. He offered to buy it from the sculptor and carried the eagle back home to his farm, giving it pride of place for all to see. It was the same lump of wood, but it took someone with insight, love and patience to release its potential.

It doesn't matter what material God has to work with. It doesn't matter how polished or how ugly it is; he can take it, mould it, shape it and release what he desires it to be. Your background, upbringing, culture, nationality, history or colour is no barrier or obstacle to God. Once it's placed into the hand of the Great Sculptor, he can produce something that can amaze and bless the world.

You were born for a purpose. You were born with a predestined plan from God, and whatever stage of life you are at, God is able to take the good, the bad and the ugly and work it into something amazing. Life is not a patch; it's a quilt. The desire of my heart is to encourage those of you who may be going through a bad patch to step back and see the big picture.

Satan wants to convince you that the bad patch you are going through right now is your lot for the rest of your life. He wants to convince you that your destiny is finished and God has no more purpose for you. It may be bereavement, divorce, a failure, a mistake or even a sin, but Satan will seek to convince you that you're too unusable, too unforgivable, too devastated, too destroyed. God says: step back and see that your life is more than just a patch in a quilt. He's able to take the good patches and bad patches, the bright colours and the dull colours, and, with the thread of his sovereign predestined plan for your life, sew them together to produce the quilt of your destiny. Look at what Romans 8:28 says: *'And we know that all things work together for good to those who love God, to those who are the called according to his purpose.'*

Nothing in life is wasted. God can and does use everything you give him – the hurts, disappointments, mistakes and failures – and somehow he amazingly embroiders these experiences into the tapestry of your destiny.

What the devil has designed to cause a stink in your life, God uses as fertiliser to produce new growth. The seasons in our life that we thought were pointless, God used as preparation material for where we are right now. David killed Goliath and became famous in a day. He was elevated from shepherd boy to national hero in one afternoon, but the process of preparation God had planned for David was essential for him to secure his victory.

Using this incident in David's life, I want to show you how God prepares us using everything in our past to see victory in the present. Right now, whether you believe it or not, God is preparing you for the next season of your life. One thing is certain: your life, calling and destiny have not only been predestined and sovereignly designed, they have been meticulously prepared.

CHAPTER 1

The Power of Preparation

I recently preached to the workers in my church a message entitled 'So you want to see Goliath's sword!' It was based on *1 Samuel 17:54: 'And David took the head of the Philistine and brought it to Jerusalem, but he put his armour in his tent.'*

My imagination ran wild as I pictured David's peers watching him in action. Young men standing on the hill overlooking the valley of Elah observing a young man, the same age as them, fearlessly and against all the odds challenging and defeating a nine-foot-tall, fully armed and trained man of war – with a stone and a sling.

People ran to their local golf store to buy golf clubs after seeing Tiger Woods produce logic-defying shots against incredible odds to win major tournaments. Youngsters ran to their local football field along with their friends after seeing a young, unknown footballer, playing in a 'nothing' team, score a hat-trick against the world champions. They all wanted the success of their heroes. They all wanted the adulation that their heroes received for their achievements. They all wanted the thrill of the victory that their heroes experienced. But in the excitement of the moment, we often forget that the victory our heroes have won did not happen by accident.

Such people forget that Tiger Woods started to play golf when he was three! Many of their football heroes cleaned football boots and scrubbed toilets before they ever ran onto a football field as a professional footballer. We must never forget that great victories are always preceded by intense preparation.

Yet all these pale into insignificance as we see David, a young shepherd boy, not only defeat Goliath but threaten the whole Philistine army. Consider these powerful words: *'For we are his workmanship, created in Christ Jesus for good works, **which God prepared** beforehand, that we should walk in them' (Eph. 2:10).* Also look at *Psalm 139:16: 'Your eyes saw my substance, being yet unformed. And in your book they all were written, the days fashioned for me, when as yet there were none of them.'*

When this revelation hits you, it will give you an incredible incentive to face your future. Moses stands before a burning bush after forty years of wondering, after forty years of condemnation and thinking 'I've missed it, I've failed, how could I have been so stupid, how could I have been so cowardly and run from my responsibility, my calling and my people?' As he stood before that bush, in the backside of a desert, in just a few moments God made sense of his past and gave him hope for the future. How? By showing him that the forty years in Egypt and the forty years in the wilderness were all part of the preparation.

Many people feel like Moses: forgotten, failed and useless. No! This book could be your burning bush – a call from God to tell you nothing is wasted. Everything can be used to prepare you for what he has called you to do. God even prepares for our mistakes; nothing takes him by surprise. Look at this verse: *'Now the Lord **prepared** a great fish to swallow Jonah' (Jon. 1:17).*

That **'prepared'** fish saved Jonah from his own rebellion and backsliding. The fish for you could be a spouse, a friend, a circumstance or your fellowship. It may well be this book. God has invested too much in you to let you be destroyed, even by your own mistakes and selfishness.

Right now, do what Jonah did and get back on course. Instead of blaming other people or circumstances for your present situation, instead of blaming God for apparently not being there for you, and instead of pummelling yourself with condemnation and self-pity, begin to give thanks. In *Jonah 2:9* we read: *'I will sacrifice to you with the voice of thanksgiving; I will pay what I have vowed. Salvation is of the Lord.'*

It's time to check out of 'Fish Hotel', repent of your backsliding, forgive yourself for your mistakes and thank God that his love and interest in you is so amazing that he even prepared for your mistakes. Give thanks now and begin to realise the destiny you were designed for and prepared for.

God is waiting to speak to your fish. I'm not an expert in biology, but I do know there were only two ways out of that fish. Thanksgiving will get you to come out the right way. *Jonah 2:10* tells us: *'The Lord spoke to the fish, and it vomited Jonah onto dry land.'*

Come on! God has been preparing you all your life. Yes, even right there in the consequences of your mistake. *'In everything give thanks; for this is the will of God in Christ Jesus for you' (1 Thess. 5:18).*

Jesus is our supreme example of the preparatory work of God. In Jesus, God shows us how we can be encouraged to discover, yield to and walk in our prepared destiny.

- His body was prepared. Just as *Hebrews 10:5* tells us: '*A body you have prepared for me.*'

- His family was prepared. Visits from angels prepared a couple to raise him and parent him.

- His ministry was prepared. Zechariah and Elizabeth were promised a son, and even he was born with a purpose: a purpose that was explained as his father prophesied, '*And you, child, will be called the prophet of the Highest; for you will go before the face of the Lord to prepare his ways*' *(Lk. 1:76)*. A ministry John fulfilled, as he was found crying out in the wilderness, '*Prepare the way of the Lord, make his paths straight*' *(Lk. 3:4)*.

May I encourage those of you who know God has something special for you to do? When it comes to the development and exposure of your ministry, God is the best PR you can have. You don't have to be in the right place at the right time with the right contacts. You don't have to lower yourself to manipulate, scheme, flatter and manoeuvre. God always has someone to prepare your way. Never put yourself in a place where the grace of God can't keep you. A gift will always make room for itself.

After I had spent seven years travelling as a youth evangelist, ministering in schools, youth clubs, churches, on street corners and anywhere and everywhere God opened doors, God instructed me to plant the church I now pastor – The King's Church, Newport. Although I had little pastoral experience, the church grew immediately, and within the first year around eighty people were meeting together regularly, in itself a great season of preparation for future challenges!

During this time there was one man whom I greatly admired and wanted to meet. He was Pastor Ray McCauley – pastor of the Rhema Church, Johannesburg, South Africa. I liked his preaching style, his manner, his way of building the church, his balanced message on prophecy and healing, and I considered that time spent with him would be very beneficial as I sought to build my own church. In 1990 I was asked to speak at the Elim Pentecostal (National) Conference. Having accepted the invitation, I planned to travel on the Monday, preach at one session and then return home before lunch the following day. This way I would be able to attend the church's weekly prayer meeting.

As I was looking through the brochure that detailed the week's programme, I noticed that Ray McCauley was due to preach Tuesday lunchtime to pastors and leaders. I was now sensing the Holy Spirit prompting me to attend that service. Although having planned otherwise, I couldn't get away from the Holy Spirit's gentle prodding to stay. After a little 'bargaining', I said, 'Lord, if I go, please would you arrange for me to spend a few minutes with Ray McCauley, so I can ask him a few questions about building a local church?'

As I went to the meeting and sat among the eight hundred delegates, I was still feeling a little bit uneasy that I'd been bargaining with the Holy Spirit. However, I took my seat somewhere in the middle of the hall and away from the platform at the front, just another face in a sea of faces.

As Ray McCauley began to preach, I could feel God giving me a spiritual song. This in itself was not unusual, as God has often used me as a psalmist to sing prophetically to encourage and release God's people, but as I started to rehearse the song in my spirit, the Holy Spirit told me that Ray McCauley would call me to go forward. God's instruction was clear: 'Go and share the song I have given you.' At that moment, Ray stopped preaching and called my name from the platform. 'Ray, come here.' I looked behind me to see if he was pointing to someone else. This was unusual, not least because I had never met Ray personally before this. I had no idea how he could possibly know who I was.

As soon as I realised he was actually calling me, I knew the Holy Spirit had prepared me with a song. I walked onto the platform and took the microphone from Ray. As he handed it to me, no words were exchanged; I simply sang the song, handed the microphone back to Ray and sat down. God's power was released and many were set free. As for me, I just sat there thinking, 'What was that all about?'

Afterwards, Wynn Lewis, the pastor in charge of that particular service, asked me if I would like to accompany Ray McCauley and him to lunch. I knew then that God was setting me up with something much more than I had asked for. Instead of the ten minutes I had so earnestly desired, I was rewarded with two hours with Ray. He shared with me how he had learned about my ministry from Reinhard Bonnke and that he had heard me sing at the 1988 Fire Conference in Birmingham, but not only had he heard of my ministry, he was waiting for the opportunity to talk to me and invite me to visit South Africa to preach at his church, and to minister at his annual conference the following year.

Since then, Ray and I have become close friends, and he has had great input into my life, especially with regard to helping me to fulfil my destiny as pastor of the King's Church.

God is your best PR. Let him arrange your life-changing encounters. Just as John the Baptist was raised up to prepare the way for the Lord and to make his path straight, so God will raise up people and bring them into your life. He will prepare your path and make it straight. Right now, cease from your fretting; stop trying to kick doors open and trust him.

The most amazing thing about God's preparation is that it is so thorough. I have discovered that not only has he prepared a destiny for me, he has also prepared me for that destiny. As I look back over my life, I now realise that my upbringing, my personality, my temperament, my talents, my experiences and even my disappointments have all been woven together to fit me for my predestined purpose on earth.

Jesus' life was prepared for him: he always walked in his Father's prepared tomorrows. He knew that a colt tied to a post just outside Bethlehem had been prepared to transport him into Jerusalem. He knew where to send the disciples and knew that the availability of the colt was part of his Father's prepared plan.

The Last Supper with his disciples is another wonderful demonstration of the way Jesus' life was prepared. He sent his disciples to prepare for the Passover. They asked the obvious question: 'Where?' He said to them, *'Behold, when you have entered the city, a man will meet you carrying a pitcher of water; follow him into the house which he enters' (Lk. 22:10).*

To return to the narrative of David's defeat of Goliath, if I had been in David's shoes and a young man had run into my tent shouting, 'Show us Goliath's sword! Show us your spoils! Show us your victory!' I would have held up the sword in one hand and God's personal preparation for my life in the other and replied, 'You want to see the **fruit** of my victory but I want to show you the **root**! You want to see my **celebration** but I want to show you my **preparation**! You only saw what God did **with** me in public. I want to show you what God did **in** me in private!'

As I gaze at the men and women whom God has given me to mentor, and as I review my own personal journey to this point, I want them to reach their full potential and discover their God-given destiny; but

I want to spare them the pain, the disappointment and the sometimes weird preparatory process. However, in so doing I would be doing them a disservice, giving them a false sense of security and a distorted picture of how God views success.

As I studied David's life up to the point where he took Goliath out, I discovered that he displayed four essential qualities that allowed God to embroider what was needed into the fabric of his life. I believe we need the same qualities. We need the same attitude of submission in our lives if we are going to experience the victories we desire. We will examine these qualities in greater detail in the coming chapters.

CHAPTER 2

The Power of Patience

In *1 Samuel 16:11-13* we have the account of David's calling and anointing. What an amazing day! Unexpectedly called in from the fields, embarrassingly made to stand before the great prophet Samuel, and then to feel the anointing oil flow through his hair and down his face. What an experience! What an honour! What a potential future!

David did not immediately run out to find a PR company to publicise the event. He didn't print publicity leaflets declaring his special anointing. He received his call humbly, went back to his responsibilities looking after his father's sheep and waited patiently for God to work it all out.

Is that where you are right now? You know God has called you to do something. It may not be as spectacular as David's destiny, but deep down you know God has put his hand on you for something. I knew quite early on in my Christian life that God had called me for something special, but it took many years of cooperating with God for me to walk in that calling.

As David waited patiently in his calling, trusting God to reveal what he needed to know at each step, God began to manoeuvre, mould and orchestrate events to bring his anointed one to the place where he wanted him. As you follow David's example and wait patiently in your calling, you will notice a process. We can divide this into a number of steps:

Step 1: God will open doors for you

(1 Samuel 16:17-18a)

This is a lesson we must all learn if we are going to walk in our pre-planned destiny. Don't kick doors open: wait for God to open them.

During the 1980s God opened a door and used me to reach thousands of young people all over the UK and Ireland; but it wasn't a door that I kicked open. It was a door that opened entirely through the orchestration of God. At the time I was working in a youth club in my home village of Resolven, South Wales, a little place of around three thousand people. Having become a Christian in 1971, I had been serving God in a local Pentecostal church. I had been a Sunday School teacher, sung, testified and from time to time preached there. (I still have a tape of one of my first sermons: I sometimes play it to people who, having started to preach, feel like giving up. After listening to the tape, somehow they seem to think their preaching is not so bad and are encouraged to keep going.) By 1980 I already knew that God had called me into a season of work with young people, and so I took a job working at a youth club. I spent a wonderful twelve months there, but little did I expect God to do what he did.

A young man who attended a private school in Swansea, who had heard me sing and speak at the club, asked if I would go to visit the school and sing at their morning assembly. My initial reaction was that not only had I never done anything like that before, but I could only play three songs on my guitar – and those songs were not exactly the type of songs fourteen- to eighteen-year-olds listen to.

Having been convinced that I was good enough, I agreed to go. I walked onto the platform, wearing black velvet flares flapping nervously in the breeze (definitely not in fashion in 1980) and armed with my three Christian songs and a guitar plastered with Jesus stickers. The next fifteen minutes were the longest fifteen minutes of my life. When I had finished, I walked off the platform thankful it was over and having changed my request to God to go into the ministry.

I had also agreed to do a lunchtime concert the same day, though nobody there seemed to realise they would have to sit through the same thing twice. The longest fifteen minutes of my life were followed by the longest morning! As one o'clock came, I dragged myself to the hall where the concert was to take place, comforting myself with the thought that after the earlier performance no one would be there. I walked into the hall and found to my amazement it was packed. I thought I had gone to the wrong place, but sure enough they had come for the concert. Again, armed with my marvellous fashion sense, my Christian songs and my Christian guitar, I launched into what I thought would be my first and last concert. The audience listened graciously and at the end I invited anyone present who wanted to receive Christ to respond openly by raising their hands. I could not believe my eyes – over half the people present openly indicated their desire for salvation. The headmaster, who was a born-again believer, invited me to stay in the school for a whole week, talking to the young people about my faith. During that week, many scores of young people responded and a wide door of opportunity opened up for me as requests to visit other schools started to arrive. Those fifteen long minutes became ten years, as God used me as an evangelist and I travelled all over the UK and Ireland, seeing literally thousands brought to Christ.

It was exactly the same as the way God had opened the door for David, manoeuvring him into the place he wanted him to be. God did the same for me and he will do the same for you. He may be opening a door for you right now. Don't be afraid! Don't think you can't do it! Don't listen to the opinions of others! Go for it! And you will be surprised what will unfold as you obey.

Step 2: God not only opens doors, he also equips you for the job he wants you to do

God knows when you are ready to be used: trust him. I did not feel I was ready for that school assembly, but God did. David did not push himself into Saul's court: God opened a door. David didn't display his attributes. *1 Samuel 16:18* **is not what David said about himself, but rather what others said about him**. One of Saul's servants said, 'I have seen.' God will equip you for the job, but don't believe your own publicity. Let others see and recognise God in you. This verse says that David was a skillful musician, a man of valour, a man of war, a man of character and charisma, and most important of all, God was all over him. God will equip you for where he has desired to send you. He will endow you with your particular gifting to fulfil your particular calling, but make sure you are not the one to declare it and publicise it: **let others see it**. As for you, don't esteem yourself more highly than you ought, or you will stop being usable. **Humility is not thinking less of yourself, but rather thinking of yourself less**.

The reason why God could use David so mightily is revealed in *1 Samuel 16:20*. In response to the message from Saul to send David to him, we are told, *'Jesse took a donkey loaded with bread, a skin of wine, and a young goat, and sent them by his son David to Saul.'* David didn't come on a chariot displaying his attributes, he came on a donkey carrying what his father had asked him to bring. Wonderful! Let God open doors for you. Let others see what God has given you.

Step 3: God will give you favour

(1 Samuel 16:21)

Saul received David with open arms and gave him the favoured position of armour-bearer. As you wait patiently in your calling, you don't have to flatter people to get where you want to go. There is no spirit of manipulation or bribery in your life. If God has called you, not only will he open the right doors and equip you with the necessary means, but he will also supernaturally give you favour with the right people.

Step 4: God will anoint your ministry

(1 Samuel 16:23)

When I walked into that school at 9 a.m. I did not feel any anointing. I had plenty of feelings, but anointing was not one of them. When I walked away from that school a week later, with hundreds of young people won to Christ, I realised God had supernaturally anointed me to do what he had arranged and orchestrated. He always provides where he guides. God will never anoint you in a place you put yourself. So be encouraged: if God has opened a door of opportunity for you, he will equip you. It will be recognised by others, and there will be an obvious anointing to do the job.

Step 5: Never forget where you came from

(1 Samuel 17:15)

In *1 Samuel 17:15* there is a beautiful statement that shows us the wonderful way David handled all that heady stuff. Taken from the fields where he had been tending sheep, anointed and separated by God in front of his whole family and serving as armour-bearer to the king made David a prime candidate for a Humpty Dumpty ministry. But David did something that demonstrates to us a wonderful principle, one that will help us face and deal with the cancer of pride. He never forgot where he came from: *'But David occasionally went and returned from Saul to feed his father's sheep at Bethlehem.'*

Although David's ministry was taking off and God was opening doors, giving favour, supernaturally equipping and anointing, he occasionally returned to where it had all begun. He returned to the few sheep bleating in his father's fields. The realisation of where God had brought him from would keep him humble, and as a result God could find him usable. **David didn't draw his self-worth from what he did, but from who he was**. He didn't feel he had to stay in the limelight to feel good about himself. He realised it was more important to be usable than to be used.

My conversion was dramatic. God spoke to me in a cinema and saved me from a life of drugs, sex and rock and roll. One result of having such a wonderful testimony is that I soon became quite a celebrity in Peniel Temple Pentecostal Church. The pastor was so excited that I was frequently asked to give my testimony, but before too long the novelty wore off and I was no longer 'flavour of the month'. Being a young convert, I soon became confused and felt rejected, unable to understand why it was that I was no longer asked to give my testimony. Confusion and rejection led to jealousy of others who had been asked to testify instead of me, and discouragement followed because suddenly I no longer felt as important as I had been made to feel. Little did I know that I was getting ready to learn one of the greatest lessons of my Christian life.

My youth leader at the time could see what was happening to me and sought to address the issue. He sat me down and told me of a TV programme that he'd watched the previous night. Initially not understanding the purpose of the conversation and the reason for his recounting of the story, I simply listened, confused and hoping he would 'shut up' – but he didn't. He continued to explain about this medical programme that showed a surgeon performing open-heart surgery. Having explained graphically the whole messy surgical procedure, he said, 'Ray, I noticed that when the surgeon finished with one instrument, he simply placed it on the table and asked for another instrument. The instrument that was on the table and the instrument that was in his hand had the same value. The instrument on the table didn't drop in value because it wasn't in the surgeon's hand; it just wasn't needed at that time.' He looked at me and continued, 'Ray, whether you're in God's hand or on the table makes no difference. It's not being used that gives you your value, it's being usable.' Wow! The penny dropped. I was set free from performance-based Christianity. Whenever the swell of pride from being used or the sting of rejection from not being used arises, I remind myself: my value doesn't come from what I do, but from who I belong to. I would advise you that as

God begins to open doors, gives you favour, anoints and uses you, you should do what David did – occasionally return. Never forget where you came from.

CHAPTER 3

Patience Will Help You - 'In Between'

The time between the anointing by Samuel and the summons from the palace to serve Saul isn't evident in the Bible account, but I'm sure it wasn't the same day. I'm sure there was some time between the calling and the first open door. God does more in us when we're 'in between' than at any other time. Some of you are **'in between'** right now. God doesn't translate us straight from A to Z; he transforms us by leading us through the whole alphabet in between – and if that is where you are right now, things may not make sense!

The experience I shared in the previous chapter showed that I was **in between** being used and not being used; but it was while I was **in between** that I learned that great lesson about value and personal worth. It's the **in-between** times when things seem to come to a standstill. It's the **in-between** times when things can actually feel they're going in reverse. It's during the **in-between** times, when there seems to be nothing happening, that God is doing the greatest work in us for the next season or door of opportunity.

I recently read a wonderful book called *Secrets of the Vine*, written by the author of *The Prayer of Jabez*. In this little book Bruce Wilkinson beautifully describes the conversation Jesus had with his disciples at the Last Supper *(Jn. 14)* and the wonderful teaching on fruitfulness found in *John 15*. As I read, I realised there were some things I'd never seen before and it opened up a whole new area of understanding that has changed my life. In John 14, Jesus met with his disciples for what we know as the Last Supper, but for the disciples it was a Celebration Supper. Mr Wilkinson beautifully describes the scene:

It was the night before Passover, Jerusalem was packed with thousands of excited, expectant Jews. Would this be the Passover that Messiah would come? The Disciples knew something the others didn't. Messiah had come! He was with them! He was already there!

Tomorrow His Kingdom would come! Tomorrow would be the most exciting day of their lives. Tomorrow, thousands of angels would descend from Heaven and teach the Romans a lesson they would never forget. Tomorrow, God's glory would be revealed, Jesus would be crowned King and they would sit in honoured positions alongside Him, in the new Kingdom. This was not the Last Supper for them. They entered the Upper Room that night with a mindset of victory, rejoicing, excitement and expectancy. Then suddenly, the whole atmosphere changed, as Jesus began to talk about betrayal, denial, pain, defeat, rejection and departure. The final shattering blow that demolished their dreams and crushed their future was Jesus opening His mouth and saying, 'I will no longer talk with you, for the ruler of this world is coming...' What? They thought He was going to be declared the Ruler – tomorrow. This could only mean one thing – Jesus is not going to be King. There would be no glory prepared for them. There would be no good times ahead. There would be positions for them!

As the disciples sat reeling from these new revelations, their emotions running wild like chickens chased by a hungry fox, their minds trying to make sense of what they perceived to be a change of plan, Jesus uttered words which have exploded in my spirit; words which were like a divine key placed in my hand to unlock a truth that would answer many of the questions that along with the disciples I constantly asked. The words *'Arise, let us go from here.'*

As you read these words, you may be going through a similar experience to that of the disciples. Your dreams for tomorrow have been shattered, your emotions are crushed and your hopes devastated. What you thought was the plan has been obliterated. Everything you have believed in has disintegrated before your eyes. You feel it's over. No, my friend, it's only just begun! Jesus is about to show you things related to your unique destiny, but before he can, you must obey his words, to *'arise and go from here'*.

Arise, let us go from here. I want to take you from this place of false perception of God's Kingdom to the truth of God's Kingdom. I want to take you from your perception of success to God's perception of success. I want to take you from shallow Christianity to real Christianity. Perhaps your perception of success has been status, prosperity and results. Perhaps your perception of growth in God has been that it comes pain-free, problem-free and price-free. Perhaps your perception of yourself has been one of impeccable commitment, pure motive, unswerving loyalty and model Christianity, but as life hits, God's plan kicks in and our plans dissolve in disappointment, our heart breaks at the revelation of its potential to betray, deny and forsake.

Jesus comes to you right now with the same words he spoke to the disciples: *'Arise, let us go from here.'* I want to show you that it's not about status but about service. It's not about miracles, but motive. It's not about being used, but being usable.

Eleven dejected and confused men followed Jesus down the stairs and out into the cold night air. As they continued down the hill through the winding streets of Jerusalem, the air was filled with the sounds of excited Passover worshippers. They followed on to the Kidron Valley, right up to the Mount of Olives where Gethsemane and betrayal would await. In the still of the night they stop, surrounded by rows and rows of neatly tended vines that have been bearing fruit for generations, and there, in between the Upper Room and Gethsemane, Jesus teaches them the wonderful secrets of the vine: 'I am the vine you are the branches.' These were truths they would never have understood in the Upper Room. Truths they would never have understood while their minds were filled with power and position. Jesus not only chose the subject carefully, he also chose the place to teach it. When they were in between the Upper Room and Gethsemane, when they were in between the place of broken dreams and a hopeless future, some of the greater and long-lasting lessons were learned. Where? In between.

That's where you are right now, in between something. Perhaps Job describes your condition perfectly: *'For there is hope for a tree, if it is cut down, that it will sprout again, and that its tender shoots will not cease. Though its root may grow old in the earth, and its stump may die in the ground, yet at the scent of water it will bud and bring forth branches like a plant' (Job 14:7-9).*

Is that where you are right now? Something that used to stand tall is now cut down by failure, disappointment or the circumstances of life. You remember the days when you faced life with boldness, excitement and vision, but one by one you have felt the lumberjack's axe cut into you, until finally you just felt you couldn't take any more. Disappointment took a swing at you and cut into you. Betrayal took a swing and cut into you. Rejection and bad news took a swing at you, and now what used to stand tall lies dead on the ground. You're lying there like the disciples in that place 'in between' broken dreams and a hopeless future.

I'll never be what I used to be! I'll never be what I want to be! I'll never be what I was designed to be! Not only are you cut down, but your roots have grown old in the earth. Something that used to feel the rush of life has now grown old. You have forgotten how it feels to have the rush of life pass through you in praise and worship. You have become old in your thinking. Old in your expectations of God; old in your dreams for the future; old in your passion and determination. You are resigned to your condition: this is how you will finish your life. All you have is numerous memories of what used to be and wishful thinking of how it could have been. Like Job you cry, *'Oh, for the days when I was in my prime . . . and the rock poured out for me streams of olive oil' (Job 29:4-6, NIV)*. Where once was a passionate, hope-filled heart, now there is a tree cut down, whose roots have grown old in the earth and whose stump is dead in the ground.

Is that how you feel? Well, I have some good news for you. It's not over, it's just beginning. God says, 'There is hope for a tree if it is cut down that it will sprout again . . . at the scent of water it will bud and bring back branches like a plant.'

The disciples were like that cut-down tree. In between broken dreams and a hopeless future, they started to smell water. Jesus opened up their minds to incredible revelation regarding fruitfulness, but they were never in a better place to receive it. You may be a tree cut down, lying there, 'in between' something, but you have never been in a better place for Jesus to teach you something that will take you into the best season of your life. Smell the water: run to the Word. What is he trying to teach you? If you're 'in between' something, God is preparing you for the next level. Don't give up, don't think it's all over – smell the water.

In the midst of the worst experience of the disciples' lives, as they were still trying to deal with the disappointment of the Upper Room and the fear in their hearts regarding the future, Jesus was preparing to teach them the greatest truth. **God has chosen not only what he wants to teach you, but also when he wants to teach you.** You are never more teachable than when you arrive at a place between the Last Supper and Gethsemane – the place between broken dreams and a hopeless future. Is that where you are? You're in a place where he can show you things he couldn't show you anywhere else.

God chooses the in-between times to teach his servants their greatest lessons. Joshua was in between the call of God and the pull of his friends and passed the test of commitment. Joshua sat on Mount Sinai for forty days, halfway up the mountain, in between the glory of God where Moses had stayed for forty days, and the carnal shouts of his friends as they danced around the golden calf of compromise. But he passed the test – in between.

Moses was in between the death of a dream and the resurrection of a dream. Forty years between Egypt and his visitation. Forty years in a wilderness in between what was and what could have been; but there, in between, God developed the necessary character needed for his future. Joseph was in between rejection and respect. For years he endured rejection, betrayal, lies, false accusations and broken promises. But while in between the rejection of his brothers and the respect of a nation, Joseph learned the principles of servanthood.

Samson was in between humility and honour. As he worked in a Philistine mill, humiliated, bound, sightless, working for the enemy, an embarrassment to his people, a joke to the world, his hair began to grow and he learned the power of grace.

Job was in between the taking away of the first and the establishment of the second. As he lay there in the dust, scratching his open sores, still reeling over the loss of everything he had, right there in between he learned the power of trust.

Peter, in between failure and restoration, went out fishing, trying to forget his cowardly denial, probably feeling less than a human being. His public testimony had turned sour, yet, in between, he was being prepared to understand the power of forgiveness.

Jonah, in between rebellion and revival, was confined to a fish's belly at the bottom of the sea, as far away from his calling as he could be. Right there – in between – he learned the power of repentance and finished his course.

What are you in between? From the lives of Bible characters such as David and from my own experience, I can assure you and encourage you that the greatest and longest-lasting lessons are learned 'in between'. Smell the water: he's trying to teach you something.

CHAPTER 4

Faithful in Father's House

The next quality of David's which allowed God to use him in the way that he did was faithfulness. As I read *1 Samuel 17:17-20* I noticed that David's faithfulness in serving as a son in Jesse's household involved him passing four tests. If we are to become usable material for God, I believe our faithfulness will be tested in the same four areas. *1 Samuel 17:20* says, *'David rose early in the morning, left the sheep with a keeper, and took the things and went as Jesse had commanded him.'* This verse is packed with revelation for those who want to cooperate with God, as he purposes us to discover and walk in our destiny. David passed:

- The Passion Test – he rose early

- The Responsibility Test – he left the sheep with a keeper

- The Servanthood Test – he took the things

- The Submission Test – as Jesse had commanded

David rose early, not because he knew that this was the day he would receive national recognition and fame, nor because he knew he was about to become a national hero, but to take cheese sandwiches to his brothers.

Here is the future king of Israel, the already anointed and set apart leader of God's people, rising early, to take sandwiches to his brothers! David rose early because he was passionate to obey his father in the small things. What about you? Are you waiting for that spectacular open door? Are you saving your passion for the day when you're recognised and firmly placed into that position or ministry you know you were born for? What about the small thing God has asked you to do recently? Now? Where is your passion for that? Do you rise early?

It may not be a challenge literally to rise early, but what about figuratively? Do you rise early for that Sunday School class that God has asked you to teach? Do you rise early to witness in the place God has put you to work? Do you rise early to look after those children God has blessed you with, or are you lying in bed waiting for the big break, the international ministry and the recognition you crave? David rose early and his only audience was God. God is never going to trust you with anything great until you can show him you are just as passionate when you're doing things with only him as an audience.

A few years ago I was preparing to preach at the Hillsong Conference in Australia. Under the leadership of Brian Houston, Hillsong's conference has become one of the greatest global conferences of this generation, impacting the local church and inspiring thousands. I have had the privilege and tremendous honour of ministering at the event several times, but one occasion in particular reminds me of David's passion. Conscious of my responsibility as a keynote speaker and the thousands of young passionate people I would be addressing that night, I was preparing my heart and mind when the Holy Spirit took me back to times when I had sat in similar conferences, listening to great men and women of God preach. I knew that God had placed a preaching gift in me, but I was also painfully aware that the treasure was deposited in an earthen vessel. I would sit there, simply a face among the thousands of faces, watching and listening to the great warriors of God inspiring people. Part of me would rejoice, but part of me would be sad because I thought I could never get to where they were. I considered that God could never trust me with that sort of responsibility.

God reminded me of those times and said, 'Ray, there will be thousands of young dreamers there tonight, sitting where you once sat, thinking the thought you once thought. Go and encourage them with the lessons you have learned, the tests you have passed and the journey you have made, in order that I could find usable material.' As I thought about what the Lord was saying to me, I asked in my heart what lessons I have learned and what tests I have passed, when all I've done is to seek to obey him the best way I know how. God responded to my thoughts by saying, 'I can trust you with this great responsibility because you passed the passion test; you were as passionate about taking cheese sandwiches to your brothers as you are about slaying Goliaths; you were just as passionate standing in front of a handful of teenagers in a school at 9 o'clock on a cold November morning as you are now, about to preach to twelve thousand people.' My heart began to fill with joy as God encouraged me to realise I'd passed some tests, especially the passion test.

That night I shared with the people the basis of my conversation with the Lord that afternoon and exhorted them, at whatever stage of life they find themselves, to rise early, be passionate and be determined at each stage of discovery. In other words, 'Whatever your hand finds to do, do it with all your might.' I exhorted them to be as passionate as I had been, as David had been, by doing something for God when he is the only audience.

In fact, whatever we do, whether in word or deed, ought to be done with that motive – to receive the applause of heaven. I desire the same accolade that heaven gave Stephen as he was being stoned to death for his obedience. He looked up to heaven and saw Jesus standing. After the resurrection Jesus sat down, but as he saw one of his servants being faithful and passionate, with heaven as his audience, Jesus gave him a standing ovation. That is what it's going to take for God to trust you with greater things – passion, when only heaven is your audience.

Life and destiny are made up of stages; one stage doesn't start until the other is finished. When God created the earth he did it in stages; after each day was created he looked at it and said, 'It is good,' and moved on to the next day. There was still much more to create, but he did it one stage at a time.

Paul said, 'Not that I am perfected, yet I press on to take hold of that for which Christ took hold of me.' If you study the lives of people God has used, one characteristic becomes evident in them all. At each stage of their prepared destiny, as it was revealed to them, they gave it all they had. That afternoon in Australia, God reminded me of how, by his grace, I had passed the passion test at each stage of my revealed destiny. Shortly after becoming a Christian, working in a paint store and passionate to witness, I rose early. While working in a factory picking up scrap metal and putting it in a bin, I rose early.

On one occasion, at a conference, I was asked by a young man, 'What was going through your head, working in a factory but knowing the call of God was on you to preach? Didn't you get frustrated?' I answered, 'I wanted to be the best picker-up of scrap metal in the factory.' Before I left that company, as a result of rising early and being passionate to work with excellence I became a candidate for promotion to run an entire department.

Setting up my own business as a painter and decorator, I rose early and gave it everything I had. Teaching Sunday School children, preaching in the Welsh chapels, travelling with an evangelistic team in a three-thousand-seat tent and travelling as a youth evangelist for seven years, reaching thousands of young people, I rose early and gave it everything I had. As pastor of the King's Church since 1989 I have risen early and given it everything I have.

There at Hillsong, as I reviewed my journey with the Lord, I realised I had passed the passion test. Whether I was working in a factory or preaching to thousands, the secret was to do it with the determination to give it your all. Rise up early and whatever your hand finds to do, do it as if heaven is your only audience. You need to have the spirit of the Terminator, programmed to complete the mission, no matter what. There is nothing that frustrates the devil more than a Christian who is determined to complete their mission no matter what.

You may be a housewife running a home and raising children; you may be a student in school or college, you may be working in a factory just as I was and doing a mundane repetitive job, but wherever you are, whatever you are doing, don't spend your days wishing, hoping and complaining about your present situation. God is preparing you for the next season of your life. Pass the passion test where you are and God will take you to the next stage.

Because of my success at the school in Swansea, I thought God was preparing me to be a teacher. I decided to enrol on a two-year course at what was then known as a teacher training college, in order to become a qualified teacher. An interview was arranged with the college selection committee, which I attended, full of hope and expectation. At the interview, one of the professors asked me if I had any academic qualifications. When I replied that I had one 'O'-level pass in Religious Education, a patronising smile spread across his face. He glanced at his colleagues with a look that made me feel I was in the wrong place and out of my depth, leaned forward, and peered over his spectacles. As he was about to speak I had exactly the same feeling I had when my junior school headmaster was about to inflict six of the best on my rear end for beating up Michael Rees. When he spoke it was in a low, condescending voice. 'Mr Bevan,' he said, 'you need another two 'O'-levels and at least one 'A'-level before we can accept you into this college. There are only eleven months left before term starts next year, so I would suggest you think about another career.' He continued looking at me in a manner that made me feel I was sitting there with short trousers and a school cap, but there was more to come. He continued: 'This week I was visiting a friend in the local hospital, where I noticed a vacancy for a hospital porter. Why don't you apply for the job? You would probably have greater success.' His lips turned up at each side, forming such an arrogant smile that just for a moment he made me wish I was not a Christian. Something rose up inside me and out of my mouth came the immortal words, made famous by Jesus and copied by Arnold Schwarzenegger: 'I'll be back.' I promised I would return in eleven months with two extra 'O'-levels and an 'A'-level and walked out of that office with a great determination in my heart to deliver the goods on time.

When the dust settled, I realised this wasn't going to be easy. Little did I know that God was setting me up for the next stage of my destiny. I enrolled at night school, attending two nights a week to study 'O'-level English and Sociology. In addition, I asked a schoolteacher I knew to help me with the 'A'-level Religious Studies paper. She said, 'Ray, you do know the 'A'-level course is a two-year course? You have less than a year before you sit the exam. You may end up being disappointed after all the hard work!'

Having worked out a study plan that involved radical discipline of my time, I threw myself into the project with a passion. If I failed the exam, I knew it would not be for lack of dedication and commitment. The following nine months were given over to study, but what I did not realise was that God was preparing me through this disciplined study to equip me for what I'm doing right now. Every week I have the responsibility of preparing food for my congregation. Sunday after Sunday I have to bring the Word of God to feed God's people and I don't think I could have studied, prepared and delivered the Word on a constant basis without those nine months of intense study. God needed to resurrect my brain cells. He needed to show me what disciplined study was, and more importantly instill in me a love of reading, meditating and writing. Throughout this time God was preparing me not to be a schoolteacher, but a Bible teacher.

When the time came to sit the exam I found myself, at thirty years of age, sitting in an examination room with teenagers, nervously waiting for the exam papers to be placed in front of me. The 'O'-level wasn't as hard as I imagined, but the 'A'-level was a different story. I was unable to complete one question because I ran out of time; I left the room feeling I'd done my best, but was it enough? The weeks of waiting between sitting the exam and the result were unbearable. I felt that my future depended on the result: would I be starting my training as a teacher the coming September or would it be back to the drawing board? Whatever the outcome might be, I was satisfied that I had risen early, I had given it my all and I had studied earnestly. I had done everything, knowing heaven was my only audience. The day came when I was to go to the school to collect my results. I tore open the envelope, closed my eyes, took a deep breath, and then looked down. I looked specifically at the 'O'-level results: English 'B', Sociology 'B'. I controlled my emotions because the one that now mattered was the 'A'-level. I had to get at least a 'C' to be accepted. I looked down again and couldn't believe my eyes – there was a great big 'B' staring back at me. I felt so good. I felt so excited. I couldn't wait to go back to that teacher training acceptance committee, results in hand, and wave them under their arrogant noses. I think one of the driving forces that kept me so disciplined and committed during those nine months was the satisfaction I believed I would get from doing just that.

As it was Tuesday, the night of our weekly church prayer meeting. I was going to give thanks to God through prayer and praise, so everyone could know my love and appreciation of my Father for having helped me do what seemed impossible. Again, little did I know God was setting me up for the next stage of my destiny. What I didn't know at that stage was that I had passed a greater test than 'O'-level and 'A'-level. I had passed the 'P'-level – the passion test. Heaven had observed my passion during those nine months alone in my study. Because I believed God wanted me to become a teacher, because I ran to get into college and would leave everything I had and give myself to it, I received heaven's smile.

That night a team of evangelists visited our church and shared their vision of reaching the lost. As they showed slides of the circus tent they had purchased, capable of holding three thousand people, and told us their plans, something began to stir inside me. I was struggling with what I was seeing and hearing from this team and what I believed God wanted me to do. My plans were made. The next two years of my life were set out before me, but I couldn't mistake the voice of the Holy Spirit gently but firmly saying, 'You are not going to teacher training college, you're going to be asked to join this team and you are to say yes.' My spirit began to rejoice but my mind said 'Uh?' I said to God, 'If it is your will that I join this team, you arrange it.'

As the team were on their way home from our church to Nottingham, where they were based, the leader, Andrew Shearman, turned to his fellow evangelist Clyde Sandry, whom I had known for some time, and said, 'There is a guy in that church who will join our team.' Clyde agreed with Andrew, mentioned my name, and, as they say, the rest is history.

They called and shared what they felt, and instead of going to college as I had expected, I stepped into the next stage of my prepared destiny. For the next two years I toured with 'International Outreach' all over the UK, touching thousands with the Gospel. I led worship, ministered in schools and occasionally had the privilege of preaching in the Big Top.

Close to where I live are some beautiful country lanes, through which my wife Laila and I often walk. On one such occasion, I noticed that though we had only walked a very short distance, she had lovingly collected at least a dozen different varieties of flowers. I was amazed. All I saw was hedgerow, grass and trees, but she had seen something different. As we walked, she would periodically stop and curiously look under a small bush in the hope that she would discover some beautiful small flower. She held up one such flower for me to see, and with great enthusiasm and passion encouraged me to look more closely at its beauty. My response was more one of courtesy than of genuine interest, but as I gazed on this small blue flower, perfectly made, beautifully decorated and meticulous in detail, the Holy Spirit brought the words of Jesus back to my mind: *'Consider the lilies of the field.'* Now I not only had my wife on my case but the Holy Spirit too! I looked and waited for the punch line from the Holy Spirit, when suddenly he spoke to my heart: 'If you had passed by that flower, I would have been the only one to enjoy its beauty, but notice: I did not hold back in my passion to create something perfect and so beautiful in its detail.'

Wow! The thought hit me: do I hold back on my passion to serve, to minister, to create with only God as my audience? Are you a single mum giving your life right now to raising your children the best way you know how? Are you a spouse going through a season of caring for your partner, believing God for their healing? Are you a pastor faithfully serving your flock yet seeing very little growth or fruit compared to the seed you are sowing? Is what you are doing going unnoticed, unappreciated and at present unrewarded? Take courage! Consider the lilies. Even if God is your only audience, it's still worth it. Don't hold back: give it all you've got.

Right now, God is preparing you for the next season in your life. Let me encourage you. Work as if you don't need the money. Love as if you've never been hurt. Dance as if nobody is watching. **Pass the passion test** – where you are now.

CHAPTER 5

The Responsibility Test

David not only passed the Passion Test (*'he rose early'*), but he passed the responsibility test too: *'He left the sheep with a keeper.'* In his enthusiasm and excitement about doing something totally different from the mundane task of keeping the sheep, David did not run away from his responsibility. Even when he was asked to take on another responsibility, his father still expected him to be responsible for the sheep. He did not run away from responsibility to pursue something new. He did not leave things half done, did not leave his responsibility in mid-stream. If God is going to trust you with greater responsibility, you have to pass the responsibility test where you are now. What has God placed under your care? **What are you responsible for before God? However small that responsibility is, stay with it until the Father releases you from it.**

One of my biggest disappointments in ministry is leaders who have been delegated responsibility and, for whatever reason, leave situations unresolved. They leave with issues unresolved and then leave projects unfinished. People who are irresponsible in small things will never be used by God or trusted by him for greater things.

You may be in a place right now where you are tempted to leave a situation unresolved, leave with issues unresolved, or leave a project unfinished. God is not a person who starts something and then leaves it half-finished. Paul declares, *'I am persuaded the good work God has started in me he will bring to completion.'* When Jesus hung on a Roman gibbet gasping for his last breath of air, he cried out in a loud voice, *'It is finished.'* What a disaster it would have been if Jesus had submitted to the suggestion of the crowd to come off the cross and save himself. You and I would not be enjoying the benefits of our salvation if Jesus had quit mid-stream or if Jesus had given way to selfishness and said in his heart, this is too hard, I'm not really appreciated, I've got no support in this. No: that's not God. Both in the Garden of Gethsemane when he prayed, *'I have completed the work you gave me to do,'* and on Golgotha, when he cried, *'It is finished,'* Jesus shows us God is not a quitter. God does not run away from responsibility and he expects the same from us. He tells us through his word, *'My soul has no pleasure in him who shrinks back.'*

Is that where you are right now? You want to run away from your responsibility, as a husband, a wife, a pastor, a church worker, a disciple. Let me encourage you to stay with the responsibility, whatever it is or wherever you are.

Nehemiah's commitment to complete his assigned task of rebuilding the devastated walls of Jerusalem gives us a wonderful example of a man who passed the responsibility test in tough times. Nehemiah had returned to a devastated city with a God-given passion and a reinforced steel confidence to complete the assignment God had given him. The people, inspired by visionary leadership, had a mind to work. They rolled up their sleeves, restored the gates, and were halfway through before the trouble started.

Sanballat, who is a type of Satan, observed the intentions of the Jews, and before they could build up momentum he came at them with a vicious attack. His contempt and fear are revealed in the barrage of words that came from him: 'Will they fortify themselves, offer sacrifices, will they complete it in a day, will they revive the stones from the heaps of rubbish – stones that are burned?' Having surveyed the scene, Sanballat points his taunting finger, throws back his head and laughs, because he notices four areas of potential weakness in Nehemiah and his work force:

'Will they fortify themselves?

These people were no warriors. Devastation had robbed them of their fight; their seventy years of captivity had stripped them of a victor's mentality and instilled in them a victim mentality. They did not have the mentality to fortify themselves.

'Will they offer sacrifices?

How could they worship a God who abandoned them to suffer in captivity for seventy years? They could never turn to him in worship. They had no motive to worship.

'Will they rebuild the broken down walls with burnt stones?

'Look how scorched they are: these stones are totally unusable.' It was impossible for them to rebuild the city when they had no material to work with, but the clincher, the reason why it was such a joke to Sanballat, was his final question:

'Will they complete it in a day?

These people always left things half done, they didn't have the mettle, they were cowards, they ran when things got tough, they criticised their leaders, they grumbled and complained when things didn't go their way. They would not complete it.

Sanballat looked at what he saw as a bunch of feeble Jews: feeble because in his eyes they lacked the mentality, the motive, the means and especially the mettle to carry out the task. Does Satan rise up and look at the church in the same way, as he observes our lack of community, destiny and courage? Does he throw back his head and laugh at our attempts to overthrow his agenda and build God's agenda? Does he see a bunch of feeble Christians, staid in tradition, easily offended, unsacrificial people who have been that way for so long that he looks, sneers, taunts and shouts 'Will they?'

What a challenge to rise up and prove his statements untrue. Yes, life may have thrown you some bad experiences to rob you of your victor's mentality. Yes, there are some unanswered questions that rise up from within your heart: Why, God? Why did I have to go through that? Why did that devastation happen to me? These questions may be threatening your motive to worship God. Yes, as you look at your life, a life burnt by negative disappointment and abuse, you see a burnt stone – yet it is still the material God has chosen to use. The thought continually attacks you: How can God use me? I'm too burnt, I'm too divorced, I'm too sinful, I'm too mistake-ridden. Surely this is not material that God can use. Yes, you have given up in the past, turned around and run away from responsibility. Yes, you know the potential in your heart to betray, deny and forsake. Yes, you haven't got the mettle, the consistency, the determination to finish what you start. You may look at yourself and at what God is calling you to do, and feel you haven't got the mentality, the motivation or the mettle, but I want to encourage you that right now, with all hell laughing at you, you can rise up, receive God's help and pass the responsibility test.

In your heart there is a desire to complete what you have started and to stay with your responsibility, but you don't know how to deal with and overcome this feeling of hopelessness. Before these 'feeble Jews' committed themselves to rebuild the walls and stay with the project until it was completed, they had to face, deal with and overcome Sanballat's most powerful weapon.

There is an old story that describes Satan calling his demons together to plan an attack on a Christian who was refusing to quit. Satan displayed all his weapons before them, encouraging the hordes of demons to take and use them without mercy. As the demons squirmed around the array of hell's seemingly endless arsenal, they spied the weapons of division, bitterness, compromise, jealousy and hatred, but one demon in particular made a dash for a vicious-looking weapon. Unable to spot its label, he asked 'What is this one used for, master?' The devil was quick to reply, 'That one is not for sale. I use it personally. It is so successful that after I have bludgeoned the enemy with it, the door will be open for you to come in and use all the others.'

As the demons buzzed around inquisitively like a swarm of bees, Satan slowly and deliberately turned the label towards them, and there in bold letters they saw the name on the weapon: **'DISCOURAGEMENT'.**

Has Satan used it on you? His desire is to cause you to give up, turn back and stop what you are doing. May I expose Satan's tricks and the schemes he uses to get you to a place where his weapon of discouragement is most effective? Here they are:

Firstly: persistent unchanging problems

These are the circumstances of life that stubbornly refuse to change and defiantly refuse to stop coming. The Bible says, *'Hope deferred makes the heart sick.'* Another translation of *'hope deferred'* is *'unrelenting disappointment.'* Just as with Job, it is not just one message of bad news, it's not just one unfortunate circumstance, it's more of an unrelenting onslaught.

Secondly: rejection, criticism and betrayal

Satan uses this form of discouragement, and often with great effect. All Satan seemingly needed to use to stop Jesus was a Judas, a Palm Sunday friend and a Pharisee. A betrayer, a compromiser and a judge. A kiss, a turned shoulder and a pointing finger. If Satan can get you to harbour resentment, unforgiveness, bitterness born out of betrayal, rejection and criticism, he has won a decisive battle. **If Jesus had died with unforgiveness in his heart, none of us would be here.** In the face of rejection, betrayal and criticism, Jesus completed his mission. He overcame discouragement by responding with a forgiving heart, *'Father, forgive them.'* As he looked out from the Roman cross, the object of torture and death, his hands nailed, his feet fastened, his body broken and battered, he surveyed a pathetic scene. People that he had healed, discipled and loved now turned their backs, hurled their insults and rejected his pleas.

What was his response that so displeased hell and smashed Satan's weapon of discouragement? *'Father, forgive them.'* **Them**! Those I see who once laid palm leaves at my feet. **Them**! Those who once embraced me in gratitude for healing. **Them**! Those who once sat for hours with excited hearts as I taught them the truth of your Word. Those who promised unfailing loyalty and commitment. **Forgive them!**

We all have '**them**' in our lives. Is that where you are right now? Nailed to a cross by the words and actions of traitors, compromisers and judges. Nailed to a cross by the rejection of family and friends. Satan screams in your ears, 'How could they? They said they were your friend, how could they use your vulnerability as their opportunity? How could they slander your reputation, shatter your trust and leave you for dead?' Don't give in to the unrelenting words of discouragement: walk in forgiveness, trust God and move on.

My wife shared with me a story she had been told by a friend, a psychiatric nurse. On his first day at work, he noticed an old lady walking aimlessly up and down the hospital corridor repeating the words, 'How could he? How could he?' After some time he stopped her, looked into her empty, sad eyes and asked her why she continually repeated the question. She stared blankly back at him, slowly turned away and continued her daily routine up and down the corridor, repeating, 'How could he? How could he?' The young nurse, still bewildered, asked a doctor why the old woman behaved the way she did. The doctor explained that many years before, she had been a happily married young woman, but her husband had an affair and left her for someone else.

When he left, something snapped in her brain and from that day to this, all she can utter out of her mouth is, 'How could he? How could he?'

If Jesus had allowed that thought to fill his heart he would never have been able to defeat the devil and be free of his evil plan. *'Father, forgive them'* he cried, and we must do the same. They **did** hurt you. They **did** betray you. They **did** reject you. Forgiving them doesn't make them right, but it does set you free. Forgive **them** today and move on and finish what God has given you to do.

Thirdly: God's delays could be a means of discouragement.

Mary and Martha could not understand why Jesus delayed in coming to heal their brother. Similarly, in your life there may be unanswered prayer, longstanding problems and unmovable obstacles that frustratingly remain unchanged. Trust God even when you don't understand what he does. When the fullness of time came, God sent his Son. Trust him: he will do the same for you.

Fourthly: our assigned task could be the means of discouragement.

It was so in the case of Gideon, Jeremiah, Moses and many others who, when faced with an impossible task, looked at the odds of succeeding and the inadequacy of the material God had chosen, and simply gave up before they had started. Be encouraged: if God has chosen you, he must see something in you that meets his criteria. My confidence to do what God has called me to do is his confidence in me to do it. That should be enough for us. Yes, we feel inadequate. Yes, we feel unqualified. We are supposed to, because when we are weak, then he can become strong.

Fifthly: our track record can be a major source of discouragement.

Satan has a field day resurrecting forgiven sin and past mistakes. That has to be one of his favourite uses for the weapon of discouragement. Don't waste your present by regretting a wasted past. A prostitute brought her savings, a box of expensive ointment purchased from hours, days, weeks and even years of selling her body. That box of expensive ointment represented a wasted life, yet Jesus accepted it as she broke it open as an offering of gratitude for his unconditional love. We need to bring our wasted lives to the Master and leave them with him, realising that he takes our waste and recycles our lives so we can be salt and light in this sad world.

As you review your life, are you regretting the investment of time, money, relationships and decisions? Don't let the devil cause you to walk into the future looking over your shoulder. Only look back if you want to go there. Here is an extract from Bob Gass's book Starting Over that I'd like you to take a look at:

Recently I read something called *'The City of Regret.'* It tells the whole story.

'I had not really planned to take a trip this year, yet I found myself packing anyway. And off I went, dreading it. I was on another guilt trip.

'I booked my reservation on Wish I Had Airlines. I didn't check my

bags – *everyone carries their own baggage on this airline* – *and I had to drag mine for what seemed like miles through Regret City Airport. People from all over the world were there too, limping along under the weight of bags they'd packed themselves.*

'*I caught a cab to Last Resort Hotel, the driver looking back and talking over his shoulder the whole trip. When I got there I found the ballroom where my event would be held: the annual Pity Party.*

'*As I checked in, I saw that all my old colleagues were on the guest list: the Done family – Woulda, Coulda, and Shoulda. Both of the Opportunities – Missed and Lost. All of the Yesterdays – there were too many to count, but all would have sad stories to share. Shattered Dreams and Broken Promises would be there, along with their friends, Don't Blame Me and I Can't Help It.*

'*And of course, hours and hours of entertainment would be provided by that renowned storyteller – It's Their Fault.*

'*As I prepared to settle in for a really long night, I realised that one person alone had the power to send all these people back home and break up the party: Me. All I had to do was return to the present and welcome the new day!' Jump on the Train to Mercy City.*'

Pass the responsibility test; finish what you start. Don't quit, whatever way Satan uses his weapon of discouragement.

On one occasion the great violinist Niccolo Paganini stood playing a difficult piece of music when, with the auditorium packed and a full orchestra surrounding him, one of the strings on his violin suddenly broke and hung down from his instrument. Beads of perspiration formed on his brow, but he continued to play, improvising as he went. To everybody's surprise a second string broke, then a third. Now there were three limp strings dangling from his violin, as the master performer completed the composition on the remaining string. When he was through, the audience jumped to its feet and filled the hall with thunderous applause. As the clapping and shouting ceased, Paganini asked the audience to sit down. Holding the violin high for everyone to see, he nodded to the conductor to begin an encore. Then, turning back toward the crowd with a twinkle in his eye, he smiled and shouted, 'Paganini and one string.' With his Stradivarius beneath his chin he played the final piece, while the audience and the conductor shook their heads in amazement. Paganini: one string and an attitude that refuses to quit. That's what it takes: keep playing.

What a fantastic illustration to help us when strings snap in our life. We spend more time fretting over the strings that snap than contemplating what we can do with the one that remains. Life is ten per cent about what happens to us, and ninety per cent about how we respond to the other ten per cent. What snapped strings in your life are trying to force you off stage and cause you to live with that taunting voice in your head, shouting, 'What if'? Has a relationship string snapped? A financial string, maybe? A health string, or a dream string? If Paganini had taken time out, he would never have experienced the opportunity to stretch his skills, and an audience would have been robbed of the experience. Why are words like 'endure', 'perseverance', 'patience' and 'stand and fear not' in the Bible? To help us understand that authority comes not from what you've heard but from what you've survived. The favour of God is sometimes not deliverance from the problem but development through it. **Keep playing, even if it's on one string.**

CHAPTER 6

The Place of Wondering

Before leaving the subject of responsibility, we should consider the commitment Mary made to the angel to allow the word of God and the will of God to be worked out in her life. It paints a wonderful picture of some of the things we can expect to experience as we too make our individual surrender to our particular journey. When Mary uttered those amazing words of acceptance in *Luke 1:38, 'Let it be to me according to your word'*, she courageously gave up total ownership of her life to God. Her past, present and future were signed away, not with a signature of ink on paper but with a promise from her heart to complete her assignment, whatever might happen. With that gentle but resolved affirmation, Mary gave away her life as a willing vessel, to be available for God to do with her as he wished. She understood that God is not a rapist; she willingly gave her womb to be impregnated with the will of God, and the rest of her life would be surrendered to the working out of that assignment.

You have made a commitment to availability: available for God to impregnate you with a dream, a destiny, an assignment, a purpose or a calling. The acceptance of that assignment, and your commitment to it, will help you deal with and overcome the complexities of life.

Mary's obedience caused her to visit five different locations on what I call her 'Journey of Commitment', and each one is filled with lessons for us to learn as we make our own journey. It is not a chronological table of events that will happen to us as we journey through life, and sometimes we will be at all five locations at the same time. The order in which you visit them I do not know (these things have to be understood and applied personally), but one thing I do know: we will spend some time at each, more time at some locations than at others. But understanding beforehand that you will visit them will help you to realise that such experiences are neither strange nor unnecessary. You will have plenty of company on the journey, for you will meet people who have been there or who are visiting a certain place at the same time as you. So be encouraged, and as you journey on your particular path of commitment, allow God to mould and make you into a responsible servant.

The first place Mary visited as she journeyed on her chosen path was Egypt. I think of this as the 'Place of Wondering'. Everything was going fine, apart from maybe just a few hiccups. Jesus was born and Mary was looking forward to her task, returning to the familiar territory of Nazareth, to friends and family and the exciting but scary future of raising the Son of God. Then out of the blue, a seeming change of plan. *Matthew 2:13-14* records it thus: *'Behold, an angel of the Lord appeared to Joseph in a dream, saying, "Arise, take the young Child and His mother, flee to Egypt, and stay there until I bring you word; for Herod will seek the young Child to destroy Him." When he arose, he took the young Child and His mother by night and departed for Egypt.'* What? 'What's up, God?

You've orchestrated the most incredible event in the history of the universe, you have impregnated me with divine seed, and the baby I am holding in my arms knew me before I was born. He made the wood for the crib in which he now lies, he has all heaven at his disposal, and you're telling me to flee, to run away like a scared dog from a mere mortal. Why can't you deal with Herod like you dealt with Pharaoh, Sodom and Gomorrah, the Canaanites and Goliath? Why?'

When you hand over your future to God, you have to trust him with the details. When you sign your life away, the signature of commitment is written on a blank piece of paper – at least from our perspective. From then on, your times are in his hands and whether you like it or not, you will have to visit Egypt – the Place of Wondering, the Place of 'Why?' Mary's mind must have been packed full of whys. Why this plan, God? Why Egypt? Why allow Herod to kill all those innocent children? Why don't you just kill Herod, get rid of him, save the bloodshed? Save us the discomfort of going to a place where we are strangers. How will we survive? Where shall we live? How will I be able to take care of my assignment in a strange environment? I'm new at this, so can't you make it a little easier? How long do I have to wait for your word? You said, *'Stay there until I bring you word.'* Can't you just give me an indication of how long I will have to wait?'

Is that where you are right now? Do these words sound as if I had just read your mail? Take heart, it is all part of his plan; it is all part of your preparation. You've heard about trust, you've talked about trust and you've encouraged others to trust – now it's time for you to do it. Abraham arrived there – 'Why this sacrifice? Why Isaac?' – but he came out of his Egypt with an unmistakable trust in God's faithfulness to provide.

Joseph arrived there – 'Why this rejection, betrayal and injustice?' – but he came out of his Egypt with an unmistakable trust in God's protection. David arrived there still tasting the anointing oil on his mouth, still heady with the shouts of adulation ringing in his ears from his victory over Goliath. Now he was prostrate in a dark cave, with his hands stretched towards heaven, asking, 'Why? Why do I have to run? Why do I have to endure this? Why do I have to take care of these men? Why can't you take Saul out and put me in?' But when David came out of his Egypt, he had learned to trust God's faithfulness. Job arrived there: on Sunday things couldn't be better – his family around him, his business prospering, his health never better – then Monday came and Bam! All hell broke loose: his family destroyed, his business demolished, his health gone, his closest friends taunting him to curse God, his body crying out to die, his mind screaming 'Why?' But when Job came out of his Egypt he learned to trust God's love. Paul visited Egypt, the place of wondering: amidst the awe of revelation, the amazement of angelic visitation, the thrill of supernatural manifestation and the sheer buzz of revival, there was still a 'why' that would not go away. 'Why do I have to put up with this satanic thorn, this continuing irritating stab? This is the second time now I have asked you to deliver me from it. How long do I have to put up with it?' Paul came out of his Egypt with a revelation of God's grace. After his third appeal for understanding, he never asked again.

But the biggest 'why' in the Bible came from the lips of one who you would have thought would never question. Yes, even Jesus himself had to visit Egypt in his journey of commitment. Even he had to spend time at the place of wondering, when heaven went black and for the first time in his existence his Father's presence departed. 'Why have you forsaken me?' These were the words that poured out from his mouth, encouraging every dream-carrying Christian to realise we too can come out of Egypt trusting God's strength. Strength to fulfil what he started, strength to resurrect a broken dream, strength to embarrass hell, strength to perfect us and build into us a trust that is unshakeable in the face of the darkest hour and most terrible experience.

Are you visiting Egypt right now? Are you in the place of wondering? If so, let me encourage you. Heaven may be silent right now, but it's not deaf. You may be on Mount Moriah, dagger raised ready to kill your dream. You may be in a dungeon, falsely accused like Joseph, attacked by self-pity and ready to give up. You may be in a cave like David, destiny seemingly gone into reverse, desperately fighting off the wolves of disappointment and despair. You may be still reeling from sudden disaster like Job, everything gone in a day, your sanity under threat, your life pointless, your very existence pathetic. You may be totally frustrated like Paul, wanting to end the pressure, persecution and pain, wondering how you can survive another day. You may even feel like Jesus, wondering why suddenly it feels as if heaven is closed, God has deserted you, and from a cross you too shout, 'Why?' Whatever your particular circumstances are, whatever the climate in your particular Egypt, be encouraged: you're learning the greatest lesson of your Christian life – the incredible power of Trust.

Winkie Pratney says in his book *Deliverance from Fear*: **'Trust is faith plus nothing.'** If that is where you are, take encouragement from those who have travelled this way before you, those who have visited Egypt many times and each time realised that whatever the pressure, whatever the pain, whatever the 'why', you need to endure, be patient, wait as many have done before, until finally 'he brings you word'. Herod is dead, the period of wondering is over; it is time to move.

I've visited Egypt many times, been confused about the details of my journey, demoralised by the behaviour of people, devastated at the deceitfulness of my own heart, frustrated with the stubborn refusal of circumstances to change, but I've learned in hindsight at the end of the day that my times really are in his hand.

I have learned never to stop at the place of wondering. I've learned to trust all the qualities mentioned above but I have also learned that timing is essential. *'When the fullness of the time had come, God sent forth His Son' (Gal. 4:4)*. God is never late; he's always on time. When Mary entrusted her life to God, she handed over her times, her years, months, weeks, days, hours, minutes and seconds into his hands, and you cannot give them to a greater timekeeper. He's never early and he's never late.

Our perception of time is related to our frustration level; his perception of time is related to his divine purpose for our life. My advice to you, if you are in Egypt, the place of wondering, is to heed the words the angel gave to Joseph: 'Stay there until I bring you word.' He is the expert and he knows the timing.

Some years ago I had the privilege of travelling with Bobby Ball, half of the comedy duo Cannon and Ball, who rose to Beatle-style fame during the 1980s. Our paths crossed in a church in Wigan where Bobby was sharing his testimony. I had been asked to sing a few songs before Bobby was to speak and, having done so, I received considerable applause and shouts for more. As I walked off, Bobby was standing, ready to go on and, as we passed, he looked me straight in the eye and in his own inimitable way said, 'What are you piggin' doing? How can I follow that?' Not knowing him very well, I didn't know whether to take it as a rebuke or as a compliment. Here was my favourite comedian, one whom I had admired for years, now telling me I had upstaged him. My ego was soon deflated when after the meeting we were standing in the rain together as Bobby helped me change my punctured tyre. A friendship was forged that night which remains strong to this day, and on many occasions Bobby has been the voice God has used to convey his word to me during my stays in Egypt.

One day he called and asked if I would be interested in travelling with him throughout the UK, visiting various cities with a gospel show designed to reach the non-churched. The show was packed with music and laughter and culminated in me interviewing Bobby and giving an invitation for people to receive Christ. The show turned out to be buckets of fun, and after the tour I could hardly touch the cheeks of my face, they were so sore from the continual laughter. But it was more than fun, it was a resounding success and we saw many come to know Christ.

During a visit to Blackpool we were invited to Blackpool Tower Circus where we were able to watch the trapeze artists practise. It was fantastic: just Bobby, his wife, the band and myself. After the demonstration, the trapeze artist, sitting sixty feet up in the air, his underpants outside his tights, looked down from the perch where he was swaying gently back and forth as the clapping and applause stopped, and shouted, 'Does anyone want to try?' The clapping stopped and the laughing started. I thought that was a better joke than any of Bobby's, but the laughing soon faded away when we realised he was serious. I thought to myself, I will never have an opportunity like this again; so applying the immortal words, 'Feel the fear, but do it anyway', off I went, walking like Robocop, to the rope ladder that was my pathway to glory or death. As I climbed the ladder, the higher I climbed, the more ridiculous my decision seemed. 'You idiot,' I said to myself. 'You're always wanting to show off. Well make the most of it, it could be the last time.' When I arrived at the place of execution, the expert greeted me with the assuring words, 'You will be fine.' All I could think of as I looked down on the band, who now looked like small rodents, was, 'I'm a preacher, not a circus act.'

I thought that once I arrived at the top, he would say, 'I was only joking, I just wanted to see you climb the rope ladder.' Nothing of the sort! He was expecting me to go through with this. Completely at ease and at home at that height, he quickly explained the procedure. 'I want you to grip the bar tightly, and when I let you go, I want you to swing out once, then come back, lift your legs in case you hit the plank you're standing on, swing out a second time, come back, swing out a third time and then when you're flat out, arms extended, feet extended, you will hear me shout 'Let go.' Do it immediately, and fall into the net. He emphasised, 'You must let go when I say; timing is crucial. If you let go too soon, you will end up falling awkwardly. If you let go too late, you will end up in the next town! Trust me: I know when to tell you to let go. I'm an expert.' I looked down at my feet, standing on what seemed to be a glorified parrot perch, and tried to reach for the bar, but because I'm vertically challenged, I had to be held by my waist to grab it. My fingers became one with the bar, my heart was racing like a Formula One car, and all I could think of was the four ways I could die. Accepting God's call can sometimes be like that.

We read biographies of men and women of God doing incredible things, and from the spectator's seat we clap wildly until we decide to climb the rope ladder, grab the bar and hang waiting to be released at sixty feet. Then it's no fun any more. The expert reminded me, 'Don't forget, let go when I say.' All I could think of was, when he lets me go, the bar I'm holding is my best friend and I hope my arms don't come out of their sockets. Before I could think another thought, I was away. On the first downward swing, I felt my stomach drop to my shoes, my hands were welded to the trapeze and I was whizzing high through the air. I reached the apex of the first swing, the momentum threw my legs out, and I started to come back. 'Pick up your legs,' I thought, 'or you'll break them on the parrot perch.' I successfully manoeuvred them into the correct position, thinking as I did that I was glad of my old PE teacher and his gym classes. Out I went again, a terrified Welsh Tarzan wondering why I had ever agreed to this. It reminded me of seasons in the ministry when the romance goes and reality kicks in. As I came back and then started on my way out for the third time, I was perpendicular, sixty feet up, hands glued to the bar, heart pumping like bellows, suspended in the most unnatural position, when I heard the expert shout, 'Let go.' Suddenly letting go did not seem to be the most natural thing to do! I know the expert said let go, but my survival instinct said hang on. So I did, for the next four or five swings, until I lost count. I was stuck, and each time I reached the correct position, the expert shouted 'Let go', but each time my passion for life told me 'No'. Finally, on what seemed like the one hundredth attempt, I listened to the expert and let go. I floated through the air like a flying squirrel; everything went into slow motion like scenes from The Matrix. Finally, after what seemed like an eternity, my back felt the embrace of the net. I was safe. I'd made it down, only to start on the upward journey. I went up about thirty feet as a result of the buoyancy of the net, and having bounced about four or five times I finally found myself motionless and spreadeagled like a starfish in the net. I could hear my colleagues clap admiringly; I'd done it! I decided to leave the net Tony Curtis-style – if you have watched the movie Trapeze you will know what I mean. Hands holding the edge of the net, a quick flick of the legs, over you go, reaching terra firma and safety. I executed the flip OK, but with the net so far above the ground I was left dangling, much to the amusement of the onlookers, with three feet of air still under my feet. I let go and felt the welcoming thud of solid ground. I pretended it was just another daily adventure that I had taken in my stride; but inside my spirit was doing the River Dance, celebrating my deliverance from death.

I hope reading that story brought a chuckle to your heart, but more than that, it illustrates what happens when you have to visit Egypt, the place of wondering. You're thinking, 'Why did I accept the call? I didn't know it would be like this.' You're experiencing things you've never experienced before. It's scary, unfamiliar territory. You're lying perpendicular sixty feet up and the expert shouts 'Let go,' and everything within you cries, 'This doesn't feel right to me, so hang on.' Listen, trust the expert; it's all about timing. Jesus knows exactly where you are; he knows exactly what he's doing. He is shouting to some through those words, 'It's time to let go, trust me. It may seem unnatural to you, but I hold the clock concerning your destiny and it's time.' He told Isaac it's time to sow, when it was not the right season. Isaac replied, 'The land is in famine.' But God said, 'Let go. It's all about timing, my timing.' Isaac obeyed and reaped a harvest against all the odds. 'Moses, move forward, it's time.' 'But there is a great sea in front of me God, can't you see it?' But God said, 'Let go of your reasoning, Moses, and trust me; it's all about timing, my timing.' Moses obeyed and led the Hebrews into their future and saw their past totally cut off. The Bible is full of incidents where servants of God 'let go' at a time that seemed ridiculous to their instinct, but they trusted the expert who says, **'The success of your assignment is all about timing. My timing.'** Talk to Elijah on Mount Carmel, Joshua at the Jordan, Naaman with his leprosy, Mary and Martha at Lazarus' tomb. Whatever Egypt you're visiting right now, whatever place of wondering, however hard, scary or strange it may seem, it's all part of the journey of commitment. It's all part of the journey. 'Wait until he sends you word.' Wait until you hear the expert shout, 'Let go, it's time to move.' It is all about timing – his. One of the keys to fulfilling your destiny and continuing on your journey of commitment is timing – his timing. Is he shouting 'Let go'? Do it: he knows, he's the expert.

CHAPTER 7

The Place of Mercy

The second place that Mary visited on her journey of commitment was the Temple – the place of mercy. *In Luke 2:40-46* we read the account. Mary, Joseph and Jesus, along with a large company of people, were making their annual visit to Jerusalem to celebrate Passover. When the festivities were over, the family and their friends began to make their way home but, unbeknown to them, without Jesus: *'Supposing Him to have been in the company, they went a day's journey, and sought Him among their relatives and acquaintances.'* Here was the original script for Home Alone – remember when Kevin's mother is sitting on the plane to Paris and suddenly realises Kevin is not on board? The camera zooms in to her terrified face as she screams out loudly, 'KEVIN!' Picture Mary doing the same thing. Yet even scarier was that Jesus was not just her son but God's Son. This was her assignment, her designer label destiny, the one thing she was born for; the task assigned her by God – to look after and nurture the Saviour of the world, and she failed. She messed up. She was irresponsible concerning her assignment. So what did she and Joseph do? Give up? Beat themselves with condemnation or disqualify themselves because of their failure? No! They did what we should all do when we mess up concerning our assignment: 'So when they did not find Him, they returned to Jerusalem, seeking Him. Now so it was that after three days they found Him in the Temple.'

They returned to the temple, the place of mercy, and found their assignment waiting there to be picked up again. Oh Hallelujah! Here is encouragement at the highest level. Even Mary failed. Even Mary was irresponsible concerning her assignment, but God did not write her off. She wasted her time and that of others; it was a stain on her destiny record, but she retraced her steps, searched with all her heart, and eventually ended up at the place of mercy, where she found her life's purpose waiting.

We all need the place of mercy. On our journey of commitment we will all mess up, fail, be irresponsible and even rebellious, but if we take Mary's example, realise our mistake, retrace our steps and search for God with all our heart, we will always find our assignment waiting for us to be picked up, in the Temple – the place of mercy. Right at this moment, my pen is being propelled by my spirit that has learned to swim in mercy's oceans. The reality of grace and mercy is simple proof that God has to choose imperfect people to do his will, and wherever you have imperfection you have failure, irresponsibility and disaster.

Brennan Manning, in his book *The Ragamuffin Gospel,* says, '*The mature Christians I have met along the way are those who have failed and have learned to live gracefully with their failure.*' He states, '*None of my failures have proved terminal.*' Why, I ask? Because of mercy – God's ability not to give us what we deserve. *When* we realise God '*expects more failure from us than we expect from ourselves*' *(Brennan Manning)*, it makes serving God more real. Winston Churchill said, '*Success is never final, failure is never fatal, it's the courage that counts.*' You may be reading these words, beating yourself up because you have been irresponsible concerning your entrusted assignment. Take courage, run to the Temple – the place of mercy. Your assignment is waiting to be picked up.

Brennan Manning writes, '*What makes authentic disciples is not biblical mastery of chapter and verse or spectacular success in the ministry, but a capacity for faithfulness. Buffeted by the fickle words of failure, battered by their own unruly emotions and bruised by rejection and ridicule, authentic disciples may have stumbled and frequently fallen, endured lapses and relapses, gotten handcuffed to fleshpots and wandered into a far country, yet they kept coming back to Jesus.*' He continues, '*What is the story of my priesthood? It is the story of an unfaithful person through whom God continues to work.*'

God is more of a realist than we are. As Peter boldly, fearlessly declared his devotion to Christ, whatever the trial, Jesus faced him with the reality of his own fickle commitment and potential to fail, deny and run. 'You will deny me, Peter, you will fail me; I appreciate your swashbuckling spirit but I know you, I know your heart, I know your future, I know your tendency to unfaithfulness. But I still love you, I am still going to stick with you, and after you have picked up your assignment which you lost because of your irresponsibility, I will be waiting for you at the place of mercy. Use what you have received to bless and serve others. It's mercy that makes it possible for me to use you every day of your life.'

There are some wonderful thoughts in *James 3:1-2*: '*My brethren, let not many of you become teachers, knowing that we shall receive a stricter judgement.*' That would be very intimidating if it wasn't for the next few words: *'For we all stumble in many things.'* Hear that, as we do this thing called life, as we seek in our imperfection to carry out our God-given assignment, James the Apostle, speaking obviously from his own experience and tendency to fail, says, 'We all stumble', and not just in a few things but in 'many things' – that's reality.

Imagine this: it is the Olympic singles ice-skating final; a skater moves out onto the ice, the music starts and away he goes. His single loop is abysmal and his double lutz is a disaster, while throughout his performance he is more on his backside then he is on his feet. Then, when he comes to the climax, instead of devastating the judges with a big finale, he sits embarrassingly on the ice after an unsuccessful attempt at a triple salchow. The judging begins. The Russian judge: zero; the American judge: zero; the Austrian judge: zero; the German judge: zero; then the Welsh judge (I have to put him in: I'm Welsh!): nine out of ten. The other judges protest wildly: 'How on earth can you give him a score like that, after a performance like that?' The Welsh judge looks at the devastated ice-skater, who sits with his head in his hands wishing he'd never come to the competition, and, full of compassion, says, 'Well, it's awfully slippery out there!'

Are you the ice-skater, sitting with your head buried in your hands, wishing you had never attempted that project, entered that relationship or made that decision? Your performance has been abysmal; you sit there, an embarrassment to your world, disgusted at yourself, believing in your heart there will be no more skating for you, no more competitions, and then in the middle of the humiliation and expected judgement, mercy stands up with a score that you totally don't deserve. It gives you encouragement to try again, because it's slippery out there, or, as James puts it, 'We all stumble in many things.' It's time to forgive yourself, thank mercy for your undeserved score and get back on your skates.

One morning, while I was in the middle of showering, two verses from

Psalm 23 suddenly came into my mind, but rather strangely the words, which I know so well, came out in the wrong order. The words in my mind were *'He leads me in goodness and mercy and follows me in righteousness all the days of my life.'* These verses were spinning around in my head like revolving doors, until I actually spoke out audibly, 'That's wrong! The words are the wrong way round.' As I was trying to break the cycle and rearrange the words in the right order, I felt the Holy Spirit ask, 'Why is it that goodness and mercy follow, instead of lead?' Suddenly the revelation hit me, as mercy again stood up with an amazing score for a bad performance.

Jesus leads us in righteousness; his word is the standard, his word is the instruction book for how we live, love God, treat people, use our mouth, build our marriages, control our bodies. It is holy, perfect, right. Yet as we serve God, seek to live by these standards, hunger and thirst after that righteousness (a righteousness and holy standard God lowers for no one), there are times when we don't crack it, we fall short of the standard and we sin against righteousness. We slip, we deliberately sin, we fail, we deny, we are irresponsible, and because we know the standard, because we know the righteousness required, we stop right there in our tracks, believing the way forward in our particular destiny is now closed. We are content just to stay there for the rest of our lives, happy just to be loved by God. Then, in our devastation, as we stand weeping over our inability to please him by failing to walk in righteousness, he wipes away our tears with the finger of forgiveness and invites us to look out over our shoulder. To our amazement, we see goodness and mercy following – one has a brush, the other a dustpan, and whatever the mess, they purposefully and meticulously clean it up.

God then turns our grateful face around and smilingly says, 'Keep walking.' Then we understand why goodness and mercy have to follow **all** the days of our lives, because there will be days when we won't follow righteousness correctly, when we will fail to reach the desired standard. And as we stand there with a repentant heart, looking over our shoulder, God says, 'What mess? What failure? What sin? Goodness and mercy have taken care of it.'

To further illustrate the power of mercy, before we move on in our journey of commitment, I would like to share an incident that took place during my family holiday of 2002. We were enjoying our time together in Paphos, Cyprus, when my stepson Stian and my stepdaughter Marit decided they wanted to go scuba diving. I went along in my role as a responsible adult to make sure they were safe. When we arrived at the diving centre, we were taken aside and given detailed instructions concerning the safety procedures that are so vital in such a potentially dangerous activity. The more I listened to the meticulous procedures that had to be taken to ensure you stayed alive, the more the feelings I had had standing sixty feet up on the trapeze in a Blackpool circus tent revisited me. My stomach began to turn over and I wished there was some way I could graciously get out of it without looking a coward. No such luck, I'm afraid. Soon we were suited up and walking towards the harbour for our introductory dive. My fears were dispelled after a few minutes in the water. Holding hands with six other people, practising to breathe unnaturally in an alien environment, going through the sign language and becoming acquainted with the use of the equipment soon calmed my fears. The last twenty minutes of the instruction were spent diving around the harbour in about twelve feet of water. We examined coral and old bits of wreckage and watched amazed at the beauty of the brightly coloured fish swimming around us. I was very pleased with my performance, with how well I had done: this was easy, why did I ever fear? I couldn't wait to do it again. That's why, when Stian said, 'Why don't we go on a proper dive this afternoon?' I didn't hesitate. 'Let's do it,' I said.

That afternoon, we suited up again and I was preparing myself for a longer dive around the harbour. I thought that as we had already had the instruction all our time would be spent diving. Well, the last part was true, but as we boarded a small fishing boat and started to head out into open sea, I realised we were not going to dive in the twelve-feet-deep waters of the harbour. We were being whisked away, some thirty minutes' boat ride, into the open sea to coral lying forty to fifty feet below the surface. I knew this was going to be a slightly different experience when the rocking of the boat began to stimulate the cheeseburger I had foolishly eaten before the journey. I turned to the instructor and casually asked, 'What if you get sick while under water, with the breathing apparatus on?' He replied 'It's OK, the breathing apparatus is vomit-proof.' 'Oh,' I thought, 'that's nice to know!'

We arrived at the designated place. Stian and I put our flippers on; the instructor jumped into the water and beckoned me to the edge of the boat. As I stood there, I looked like an alien being, tank on my back, goggles over my eyes, an inflatable and deflatable suit around my chest controlled by pressing a blue button, twelve kilos of lead around my waist – designed to take you to the bottom and keep you submerged. The only sound I could hear was the sound of my own heart beating. The instructor, using sign language, told me to jump in; I knew that by looking at the horizon I would force myself to jump out, not up, and so I tried to coordinate my mind and body to obey the instructions and leapt into the water. As I came down, the air tanks clipped the metal plate I was standing on and smacked me on the back of the head, and at that point the hour's instruction I had received in the morning totally left me. I found myself flailing around in the water like a fish on a hook. I had forgotten to spit inside my goggles to give myself clear vision, and so, disorientated and sightless, I found myself being dragged by the instructor towards a weighted rope that hung from the side of boat. Again, using sign language, which I could barely see because of the misted goggles, he told me to press the blue button.

This would **slowly** deflate my body jacket, allowing the lead weight to **gradually** take me down; I also had to remember to blow my nose every metre, acclimatising my body to the depth of pressure. In a state of disorientation, I pressed the blue button **hard**, deflating my jacket in an instant. I shot down the weighted rope that hung down to the coral below so fast that I had rope burns on my hands. I hit the bottom, having forgotten to blow my nose; my glasses misted up, the lead weight fastened me to the coral, and then I found myself fighting with three feet of seaweed. The instructor arrived using the sign for 'Don't panic', but I was way beyond that stage. My breathing started to accelerate and I realised I was beginning to hyperventilate. All I could see was the mass of bubbles produced by my terrified breathing. I tried to remember what the sign was for 'I'm dying!' I couldn't remember, so I just pressed the blue button again. Off I went like a rocket, or someone shot from a cannon. I hit the surface so hard that I burst a metre out of the water like a performing dolphin. The instructor, against all the rules, left Stian on the seabed to come to my aid. As I bobbed on the surface, glad to be alive but embarrassed because I had messed up and put Stian's life in danger, the instructor came alongside me and calmed me down. I was expecting a barrage of rebuke and 'Why didn't you follow my instruction? You're the only one out of the twenty-five people on this dive that didn't do it right. Don't you know the trouble you've caused by your irresponsibility? Don't you know the lives you've put at risk? Get out of the water: my advice to you is never again put a diving suit on and never again go diving, you fool!' I didn't care what he said, I was just happy to be alive, but to my amazement, these words came out of his mouth: 'Mr Bevan, are you OK? **Do you want another go?'** What? Was I hearing right? Did I want another go after all the trouble I'd caused? After failing to follow the instructions, after putting others at risk? Again he asked, **'Are you ready to have another try?'**

That's mercy in its essence. It doesn't treat you as you deserve to be treated, it doesn't bludgeon you with 'You're useless, how could you?' While not ignoring your irresponsibility, it accepts your recognition and repentance for your failure and says, 'Do you want another go? Are you ready to have another try?' On that particular day I declined the offer, but what about you? Have you failed to carry out the instructions of righteousness? Have you been irresponsible? Have you put lives at risk? Are you the only one in your world who feels like a failure? Look over your shoulder: goodness and mercy are following you, wiping up the mess, and the Holy Spirit is encouraging you to look forward to the future, whispering, 'Do you want another go? Are you ready to try again?' If you've been irresponsible like Mary and Joseph in your assignment, your destiny, your entrusted purpose, follow their example: go to the Temple, the place of mercy, and find your assignment waiting to be picked up, so you can have another go. Meditate on *Hebrews 4:16: 'Let us therefore come boldly to the throne of grace (not judgement), that we may obtain mercy and find grace to help (not condemn) in time of need' (brackets mine)*.

CHAPTER 8

The Place of Breakthrough

I'm going to put the last three places Mary visited into one chapter, not because they lack importance in the order of priority, but because they will have more impact in their conciseness.

For Mary, the place of breakthrough was a wedding, to which she, Jesus and the disciples had been invited. Jesus was now thirty years of age and Mary had been faithful in raising him the best way she knew how. As far as we know, nothing particularly spectacular took place, there were no other angelic visitations and no audible voice from God, and Jesus performed no miracles and didn't do anything to indicate to anyone that he was special. Except for the incident in the temple at the age of twelve, when he stunned the religious teachers with his knowledge and understanding of the scriptures, the thirty years of Jesus' life were quiet years. We know very little about the day-to-day lives of Mary, Joseph and Jesus, but they must have been uneventful, because when Jesus turned up in his home town to start his ministry, his brothers, sisters and relatives were offended by the boldness of the claims he was making. 'Who does he think he is?' they declared. 'We know him, he's Joseph's son, nothing special. We were raised with him, played with him, bought furniture from him. He's just like us.'

Now, thirty years later, attending a wedding, Mary was about to experience a breakthrough in her assignment, when Jesus, miraculously and to the amazement of all, turned gallons of water into wine. This was the first recorded miracle performed by Jesus up to this point in his life, and now the fun was about to start. Think of it: after thirty years of faithfully committing herself to her assignment, raising Jesus, being a mother, enduring the routine of commitment, Bam! A breakthrough. The miracles begin to happen. As I pondered this incredible and sudden shift in Mary's life, I began to realise how God deals with us as we too seek to be faithful concerning our assignment. **The miraculous power of God is often experienced as we endure the routine of commitment.**

Dear reader, please learn this lesson as soon as you can, because herein lies the key to your breakthrough – enduring the routine of commitment. People waste their time running around, looking for miracles, chasing the spectacular and manipulating circumstances to create an appearance of success. They're always 'coming to pass'; they hate the routine of commitment and never experience what they chase. Paul encourages us in *Galatians 6:9: 'And let us not grow weary while doing good, for in due season we shall reap if we do not lose heart.'* Hear that: if we endure, just keep doing what we're doing, however mundane, boring, samey and routine it is. If that is where God put you, endure the routine of commitment; who knows, your breakthrough might be today! Don't despise the routine of commitment to the local church, your present job, building your marriage, developing your relationship with Jesus. In due time you will reap if you don't give up.

People get bored with their churches, jobs and ministries because they hate the routine of commitment. They try to live in the rush, the buzz, the thrill of something always happening. They hate the routine of commitment. They are feeling- and experience-orientated Christians, who spend their time playing the 'Wheel of Fortune' instead of enduring time on the 'Wheel of Monotony'.

Part of the process a potter employs in making a useful vessel is the placing of the clay on the wheel. Around and around it goes until finally the potter is happy that the clay is centred. Then his experienced hands will shape that lump of clay into the desired pot. The words God spoke to Jeremiah come to you right now, and if you are going to finish your course and experience breakthrough in your life and ministry, you had better heed his words. *Jeremiah 18:2: 'Arise and go down to the potter's house, and there I will cause you to hear My words.'* As Jeremiah observed the craftsmen at work, he began to understand something of how God seeks to shape us. The unformed lump of clay spinning around on that wheel for a while: no instant miracle, no sudden transformation, just the monotony of spinning around and around on the wheel. Nothing seems to be happening. Spinning around and around on the wheel of routine, the wheel of sameness, the wheel of monotony. To us, the endless spinning is boring, but to the potter it is essential. He has to centre the clay before he can begin to mould it. Learn this lesson fast.

There is something about the routine of commitment, the wheel of monotony, that centres us and stabilizes us. Many Christians are unusable to God because he can never centre them. They are always flying off the wheel. They fly off on the latest spiritual craze, the now thing. They're always flying off to another church; they're continually spinning on the wheel of fortune instead of remaining on the wheel of monotony. God can't shape you into a vessel of honour if you are never on the wheel. Many Christians stay unformed, undeveloped, ugly and useless because they fight against the ministry of the wheel in their lives. We must all pass the monotony test.

Joshua and Caleb are classic examples. Through the unbelief of a nation they had to endure the routine of commitment for forty years. Imagine that! Sometimes we can't stick sameness for more than five minutes, but here were two men burning with faith and vision, going around and around on the wheel of monotony for forty years. They were the only two who entered into the Promised Land. They were the only two who experienced their breakthrough, because they endured the wheel of monotony. They ate the same food for forty years, lived with the same people, submitted to the same leader, stayed in the same environment and believed the same promise for forty years. That is enduring the routine of commitment. That is passing the monotony test. Joshua ended up being trusted with the leadership of the nation and Caleb ended up receiving his inheritance, simply because they stayed on the wheel.

I cannot stress this enough: apart from having to relocate for genuine reasons, stay with your local church. God uses your local church situation as his wheel to centre you, test you and prepare you for greatness. Don't leave because of offence, don't run away because you're seemingly overlooked or not appreciated. If you don't settle this principle in your life you will be continually flying off the wheel, and wherever you end up, God will start the whole process again.

It is also on the wheel of monotony that the potter applies the water. The water makes the clay pliable. It is then he can firmly and purposefully press his fingers inside the centre of the clay and begin to pull it up and shape it. He doesn't start by painting the lump of clay with bright colours. He doesn't hand that shapeless lump of clay to the shopkeeper and say, 'Sell this as a drinking vessel.' The clay has to submit to the process of development on the wheel of monotony if it's to become anything of use.

The local church is the perfect vehicle through which God can make you what he wants you to be. Sometimes it's boring, sometimes it's monotonous, sometimes it's routine, but it's necessary. Unteachable Christians are like clay without water: they're impossible for God to shape. The most important season of my life and Christian development has been on the wheel of monotony. Ask any great musician, athlete, leader or writer: they will tell you the same. The qualities that helped them get where they did were developed on the wheel of practice, the wheel of training, the wheel of studying, the wheel of monotony. The routine of commitment or of giving time to something affects people differently. Kevin Gerald in his book, *Proving Ground,* describes the difference in terms of 'Wine Christians' and 'Milk Christians'. Wine Christians get better with time, Milk Christians get bitter with time. Milk Christians have a short lifespan of interest – they get easily distracted. They have a short lifespan of motivation and they run out of inspiration quickly. They have a short lifespan of confidence and their attitude begins to turn negative. They have a short lifespan of determination and they start but never finish well. Commitment curdles in the life of a Milk Christian. Consistency and perseverance curdle in the life of a Milk Christian. They do well as long as something is new to them, but as soon as something becomes familiar to them, they begin to lose appreciation of it. Subsequently, the loss of interest and appreciation leads to inconsistencies, enthusiasm dwindles and they're off the wheel, only for God to patiently start the whole process over again. Learn the lesson now: decide wherever you are right now to endure the routine of commitment, to stay on the wheel of monotony. Then having already visited Egypt, the place of mercy, you will be assured of a visit to Canaan, the place of breakthrough.

The next location to visit is the Place of Enlargement. Mary had to visit the cross. Three incredible years had now passed, in which thousands had been healed and found a new sense of purpose in their lives. Amazing timeless words had been spoken as Jesus' tongue was used as a pen from heaven to write eternal truth on the tablets of men's hearts. Religious mouths had been stopped, blind eyes had been opened, and the world would never be the same again because of this carpenter from Nazareth. Apart from a few relapses, where in her confusion and lack of revelation she received a rebuke from Jesus for trying to interfere in his God-given assignment, Mary had proved herself faithful in carrying out her task. Now she finds herself staring up at a terrific sight, her vision blurred with tears, her mind reeling with questions, and her son being treated as a common criminal. Over the three years, she had seen him take hilltops, houses, boats, beaches, synagogues and stones and use them as pulpits to preach the wonderful life-changing truths of the Kingdom of God, but here at the cross, she stood beneath his greatest pulpit and heard him declare from it forgiveness to the world, the completion of his mission and salvation to a dying thief. Those hands from which she had pulled splinters were now splintered with Roman metal, held tight by the predetermined will of God, which no human could remove. Those feet she had lovingly washed after he'd been playing in the streets of Nazareth with his friends were now disgustingly sodden with a mixture of sweat, blood and dirt and hammered tight, painfully tight, to the execution cross. Here she stood, helpless, broken-hearted, maybe even angry. This was her boy on the cross, her little one, her Jesus. A mother stood at the foot of that cross. Not just a disciple, not just another follower, but a mother. I believe Mary saw something far bigger than domestic relational life. I believe that in the horror of Calvary she saw the bigger picture. As she gazed on her son dying for the world, she realised this was bigger than just the two of them. This was bigger than mother and son. Her commitment took her to the cross, where she realised she had to share him with the world.

Although our relationship with Jesus should be intensely personal, it should never be selfishly private. The journey of commitment will take you to the cross, where selfishness has to die, and the realisation hits you that it's not just about you and him, but you, him and the world. You will see that Jesus' death is much bigger than your theology, your little world, your hurts and disappointments, church preference, pet doctrine or petty grievances. Jesus' death was not orchestrated by God so that theologians could have a job or church groups could discuss whether healing is in the Atonement or not. At Calvary, God wrote out a prescription for the cancer of sin, and unless we give it to the broken world people will die never knowing the freedom of life in Christ.

Communicating our faith in Christ is an absolute priority. To help you avoid being the type of person that would put people off, let me give you some simple, humorous illustrations from a children's programme that was very popular some time ago: *The Mr Men:* created by Roger Hargreaves.

There was Mr Bump, so named because of his continual handicap of bumping into things. There was Mr Sneeze, obviously named because of his habitual sneezing. Also there was Mr Lazy, Mr Tidy and a host of others who have become firm favourites in the hearts of millions of children. When I was considering this question, pictures of 'Mr Men' flashed through my mind, displaying characteristics that would be detrimental in any Christian witness.

First I saw 'Mr Soulseeker', always on the lookout for souls, potential converts, spiritual sheaves to put into his own personal reward book. On the outside he may appear to be very zealous, very spiritual, always witnessing, always seeking 'souls'. However, a closer look would reveal his lack of concern and interest for the person. He is not really interested in the kind of music

MR SOULSEEKER

the person likes, what he does with his spare time, how his wife and family are; all Mr Soulseeker can see is another pew filled in his church. Mr Soulseeker himself doesn't see this deficiency in his witnessing, but it is fairly obvious to others. His interest in them is merely statistical. He cannot converse in an easy, natural way: everything has to be spiritualised and related to the necessity of the 'soul getting saved'. It is not long before people begin to avoid Mr Soulseeker and so he consoles himself in his self-inflicted martyrdom for the sake of the kingdom.

Then there is 'Mr Stock', a walking spiritual bureaucrat; he walks very correctly. Every movement is rigidly executed with much carefully prepared thought. Every answer he gives to the variety of questions asked by the unconverted is frustratingly predictable. Mr Stock is quite unable to accommodate truth to each individual need. Each person he meets he places into a certain category: sorrowful, searching, backslidden and so on. Irrespective of the differing circumstances in each case, the same stock scriptural formula is given, whether the person understands or not. We could call him 'Mr Chapter and Verse', but in keeping with his own character and for the sake of homiletics and alliteration, we will stick to a name beginning with 'S'.

Next in line comes 'Mr Superior', the walking Young's Concordance. It is one thing to contain within your mind the vast resources of God's Word, but it is entirely another thing to possess the wisdom to use it effectively. There are certain things we do not know, and it is wise to realise when we witness that although our knowledge of scriptural things may seem quite comprehensive, it is actually quite limited. However,

Mr Superior will never accept this; he is merely out to win an argument. He feels it a disgrace to the cause of Christ to have to say, 'I don't know,' when in fact the only thing that has suffered disgrace is his own pride. People must feel they can come to us without being battered down verbally or made to feel inferior by our seeming superiority. They must see that we too are people, not programmed computers always turning out the correct answer.

Of course, we must be clear and dogmatic about the essentials of salvation and our life in Christ, but our communication of such truths must never come in an arrogant, self-assuring way, but humbly and graciously: *'But in your hearts set apart Christ as Lord. Always be prepared to give an answer to everyone who asks you to give the reason for the hope that you have. But do this with gentleness and respect . . .' (1 Pet. 3:15, NIV).*

MR SELF RIGHTEOUS

Without doubt, 'Mr Self-Righteous' comes high on the list of stumbling blocks to the unconverted. No chinks in his armour. He thinks he is God's right-hand man, not realising that the Father has only one right-hand man. Of course, Mr Self-Righteous has earned his position. You can check his record: absolutely spotless, or at least that's what he believes and he isn't slow to let people know, especially the unconverted. It is one thing to be blameless in our life and words before those we live and work with, but another to declare our goodness with our own lips or assert by our manner, as the self-righteous Pharisee did, that we are 'not as other men'. Mr Self-Righteous desires only to elevate himself higher. As a result, not only does he shut the door to many who feel they could never reach the standard of such self-declared impeccability, but he is also the subject of Jesus' anger. To the self-righteous Pharisees and scribes Jesus thundered out 'Woe' after 'Woe', telling them they were as 'whitewashed sepulchres'. They loaded people down with burdens so heavy that they could not carry them, yet they did not lift a finger to help them.

Last but not the least on the list of deterrents to successful witnessing is 'Mr Sunshine', the permanent advert for Colgate toothpaste. With such a fixed grin, one would think he had permanent scaffolding inside his mouth just to hold it in place. He feels he must always display the 'joy of the Lord', not realising that by his very attempt to convince people of his personal happiness he reduces Christianity to a fantasy, and life to one big joke. Instead of being able to weep with those who weep, to suffer with those who suffer, to empathise with those experiencing deep tragedy, he feels the best help is to smile, say 'Praise the Lord', and suppress any feelings that will attempt to take the smile off your face. Sooner or later, if Mr Sunshine does not realise his misrepresentation of the biblical meaning of joy, he himself will either break under the strain of attempting to manufacture spiritual fruit or turn into a 'One Emotional' zombie.

MR SUNSHINE

Mr Soulseeker, Mr Stock, Mr Superior, Mr Self-Righteous and Mr Sunshine are not strangers to us, as from time to time they emerge in our own lives. The difference between these spiritual Mr Men and the original versions is that they will never rise to great heights in the popularity polls amongst Christian or non-Christians. The other difference is that they are all related: they all have the same father, 'Mr Self'. Get rid of him, and we won't have any problem with the others who seek to render our witness to the unconverted ineffective.

As we continue with Mary's journey of commitment, we see that the fifth place she visited was the Upper Room – the place of infilling. In *Acts 2: 1-4* we have the most amazing account of something that had never taken place before. I'll let the Word speak for itself:

When the day of Pentecost had fully come, they were all with one accord in one place. And suddenly there came a sound from heaven, as of a rushing mighty wind, and it filled the whole house where they were sitting. Then there appeared to them divided tongues, as of fire, and one sat upon each of them. And they were all filled with the Holy Spirit and began to speak with other tongues, as the Spirit gave them utterance.

These verses have caused so much discussion, debate and even division. What was that experience? What were these tongues? Is this experience for today or was it only for the early Apostles to help start the church? Why don't we just simply believe the inspired words of Peter, stop discussing and start demonstrating, stop destroying and start enjoying? *Acts 2:38-39* states clearly, *'Then Peter said to them, "Repent, and let every one of you be baptized in the name of Jesus Christ for the remission of sins; and you shall receive the gift of the Holy Spirit. For the promise is to you and to your children, and to all who are afar off, as many as the Lord our God will call."'*

I could spend the rest of this book writing a convincing argument on the relevance and reality of being filled with the Holy Spirit and speaking in tongues, but I don't want to appeal to your head: I want to appeal to your heart. God has promised it and that should be enough for us to believe and receive it, just as we do salvation. As I see it, one hundred and twenty people came out of that upper room like wacky dynamite sticks. They were blasted out of their comfortable fellowship into the clamour of the streets. Multitudes came to see what was happening and were amazed not only by the supernatural manifestation of speaking in tongues, but by the incredible clear-cut message of salvation delivered with such conviction and power.

What is even more amazing is that the message preached came from the lips of one who, just a month earlier, was warming his hands at a different fire. In one month Peter experienced three types of fire. First, the fire of compromise, as he was challenged to declare his faith in Christ by a small girl yet continued warming his hands, cursing the name that had changed his life. Then the fire of conviction, when Jesus graciously but clinically ripped away Peter's pretence and challenged him to the very core of his being to pass not the theology or experience test, but the love test. Over an open fire with fish cooking right there on the Tiberean beach, Peter was brought to his knees, his failure addressed, forgiveness received and relationship restored. Now, at Pentecost, he was experiencing the fire of boldness. The fear gone, compromise nowhere to be seen, just a torrent of spiritual lava flowing out of his mouth. The Old Testament scripture, saturated with revelation, was communicated with such power that the hearers, overcome and cut to the heart, said, 'What shall we do?'

Why do we need to visit the upper room? Why do we need to be filled with that type of power? Because nothing less than conviction like that, boldness like that, revelation like that, will cut it. The disciples had been with Jesus for three years, they knew his words, they'd seen his power, but to do the job they were prepared for, information would not be enough.

There are many people who enrol for Bible School because they believe it will equip them and empower them to become evangelists, pastors and teachers. They spend two or three years studying Theology, Methods of Communication, New Testament Survey, the Minor Prophets and a score of other subjects, but while it is a good exercise and necessary, unless you have visited the upper room, received a baptism of fire and had your heart set alight with a burning desire to share it, all you will ever give is a speech.

Again I have to speak from personal experience. It is the best way I can encourage you if you have never known this baptism of boldness and the wonderful, supernatural experience of speaking in other prayer languages. I had already received salvation and new life. I can remember waking up the morning after I had prayed the prayer of salvation and looking out of my bedroom window. I know it sounds corny, but the sky was bluer and the grass was greener; it was as if I was looking at a different world.

I remember being invited to a dinner hosted by Cliff Richard. After the meal, celebrities would stand and share their testimonies, giving their story of how they became a Christian. There were many other invited guests present who weren't Christians, and Cliff thought this would be a perfect environment to share faith in a relaxed atmosphere. I just sat at the back, awestruck in the company of such famous people.

I remember, too, how during the course of the evening an actor stood up and explained with great oratory how he believed that God was a great light and that gradually through the centuries that light would get brighter and brighter until it reached every human being, giving spiritual illumination. He sat down, obviously very pleased with himself, believing he had said something very profound. Without thinking, I stood up and declared, 'That's all well and good, that all sounds amazing, but what if with all that light, no one could enjoy it because they were all blind? It's not more light that's needed, it's new eyes.' There was a long silence during which I just stood there with seemingly every eye turned in my direction, feeling totally exposed and thinking, 'Was it something I said?' Suddenly people started clapping and voicing their approval. After the meal I had the privilege of sitting down with that actor and explaining what I meant by 'new eyes'.

That's exactly what happened to me at salvation: I received a new set of eyes. I was seeing the world, myself and other people from a completely new perspective. During those initial few months of new life, I devoured the Bible and Christian books, I attended as many meetings as I could and I shared my faith the best I could, but inside I felt the need to be more effective. I had heard people speak in 'Jesus languages', but because they were more experienced Christians, I felt

I had to arrive at a certain level of maturity before I too could learn how to speak like that. During that time, an American gospel group called The New Creation Singers visited a church nearby. Every night, along with a group of people from the church I was attending, I went to the meeting. During this time, I became very friendly with them and they took a keen interest in me, so much so that they invited me to sing with them. One day, while I was in conversation with one of the band, she looked me in the eye and said, 'Ray, have you been filled with the Holy Spirit and spoken in tongues?' I knew what she was talking about and immediately replied, 'Not yet. I've only been saved a few months.' 'What's that got to do with it?' she asked. 'Well, I'm not mature enough to receive that gift, I'm waiting until I'm more experienced,' was my reply. She laughed loudly and said, 'Ray, you've got it all wrong, the baptism in the Holy Spirit and speaking in tongues is not a reward, it's a gift. Just like you received salvation as a gift, so it is with speaking in tongues and this baptism for power.' She read to me from *Acts 2:38* and also shared the words of Jesus spoken during the Sermon on the Mount *(Matthew 7:7-11)*. She said, 'All you have to do is believe and receive. Tonight my father (he was the preacher) will ask people to come forward if they want to receive this gift. Just believe it's for you and Jesus will baptise you in the Holy Ghost and you will speak in other tongues.' That's simple, I thought. Fortunately, as I was a young convert my mind had not been filled with the negative opinions of men, just the Word. I just thought that as it's quite clear in the Bible this is a gift for me, why waste time? Why miss out if it's for me; I want it. That night, when the preacher gave his invitation, I was first down to the front. I knew exactly what I wanted and he knew exactly why I had come. He laid his hands on my head and the only way I could describe it was like shaking a bottle of pop and then releasing the cork. From deep inside, like an erupting volcano, came this flow of strange words. I didn't have to think about them or formulate them, they gushed out of my mouth like water from a burst dam. The volume of my voice corresponded to the volume of spiritual water that cascaded from my mouth. It was wonderful; I can't explain it. My eyes were closed and I was oblivious to everything and everyone as I allowed the Holy Spirit to energise my whole being. The preacher started to carry me around, placing my hands on other people. As I touched them, they too were filled with the Holy Spirit and spoke in other tongues. On the way home to my parents, with whom I was still living at the time, I found it difficult to want to speak in English. Even on the bus travelling home, when asked where I wanted to go, when I opened my mouth to say 'Resolven', this torrent of tongues started again. The bus conductor thought I was drunk but I didn't care, this was incredible.

On arriving home, I decided to go straight to my room. I didn't want any dialogue with my parents as they already thought I'd lost it by getting saved. I didn't want them to consider committing me to an institution because I was suddenly starting to speak in the language of the inhabitants of Loo-Loo Land! When I went into the house, my parents were sitting relaxed watching TV. I managed to say goodnight and avoided any further interaction, went upstairs into my room, shut the door and just started to praise God in other tongues. As time went on, so did the increase in the decibel level from my voice. As my father came up the stairs, he heard me going for it in my room. He stopped, shouted down to my mother, 'Vena, you'd better get up here, he's really gone nuts now, he's shouting in Chinese!' Many people argue that speaking in tongues is the evidence of being filled with the Holy Spirit. Why get locked in to such an irrelevant argument? This gift is for you. Believe it, receive it and enjoy it.

After this experience, I can only say my Christian life was transformed. My passion for sharing my faith intensified, the conviction with which I lived my Christian life was unswerving, my boldness to communicate Christ caused much embarrassment among my friends and family. I had to learn to channel my new found boldness through wisdom.

Telling the staff at the paint shop where I was working at the time, 'You're all going to hell if you don't get saved' didn't seem to work. Although I learned to develop wisdom, I didn't diminish in boldness. I would stand on the corner of my street on Saturday mornings with my guitar and sing and preach the Gospel. On one occasion, I persuaded a group of friends to come to Neath town centre, six miles from my village, to stand on top of the public toilets and sing and testify. Why a public toilet? Well, the location was perfect, right in front of the bus station. Scores of people were standing in line, waiting for their buses. They couldn't run anywhere: they just had to listen.

To do the work God had prepared me to do, I had to visit the Upper Room – the place of infilling. For the work Mary and disciples were being prepared to do, they had to visit the Upper Room – the place of infilling. I don't care who you are, on your journey of commitment you too will need to visit this place. Don't remain closed to it, receive by faith this wonderful gift; you need it to take Jesus to the world.

CHAPTER 9

The Servanthood Test

As we return to the life of David, we recall how he had passed the **Passion Test** ('he rose early') and the **Responsibility Test** ('he left the sheep with a keeper'). He also passed the **Servanthood Test** ('he took the things and went'). Here was the next king of Israel, already anointed and set apart for his future role, passionately, responsibly and humbly taking cheese sandwiches to his brothers: *'He took the things and went'*. The things were nothing more than a bag of cheese sandwiches and a greeting. He didn't turn to his father and say, 'Hey, don't you remember my anointing day? Don't you remember what Samuel anointed me to do? I can't remember him including delivering cheese sandwiches to my brothers in my future CV. I've been anointed to deliver and lead a nation, not deliver takeaways.' One of the qualities that prepared David to fulfil his calling was a servant's heart. Whether it was delivering a nation or delivering takeaways, his attitude was the same.

The Special Olympics issued an advertising video showing snapshots of people competing against each other in a variety of events: disabled people from all over the world refusing to be locked up in a prison of self-pity and defeatism, giving their all as athletes in track and field events. One chap in particular touched my heart deeply. A group of Downs Syndrome athletes were competing against each other in a track event. The starter's gun sounded the beginning of the race and they all went running as hard as they could. At one point of the race, one of the athletes fell. Immediately and instinctively, all the other athletes in the race stopped, picked up the fallen athlete, dusted him down and restarted the race. What a spirit! We need that spirit in our churches, in our families and in our relationships – the spirit of a servant.

One of the greatest lessons we can learn is that spiritual promotion in the Kingdom of God comes through servanthood.

This is illustrated not only in the life of David, but also in the life of other characters in the Bible. One such person is Rebekah, whose story is told so beautifully in *Genesis 24*. It is the story of a Father's desire to find a suitable wife for his son. The father in question is Abraham and the son is Isaac. Abraham had summoned his servant to return to the land of the aged patriarch's birth and specifically to his people and family, among whom he was to find a wife for his son Isaac. It is a beautiful picture, but has much more depth and meaning than a mere romantic story. The woman that would be chosen would be instrumental in continuing the line that would eventually bring God into the world. What challenged me above everything else was the test this woman had to pass in order to be deemed suitable material. It wasn't a beauty test, even though she would pass such a test – *Genesis 24:16* says she was *'very beautiful to behold'*. It wasn't even the moral test, as the same verse says she was *'a virgin; no man had known her'*. No! The test she had to pass was that of servanthood. Abraham's servant, realising the importance of the choice, prayed, *'Now let it be that the young woman to whom I say, "Please let down your pitcher that I may drink," and she says, "Drink, and I will also give your camel a drink" – let her be the one You have appointed for Your servant Isaac.'*

Realising that the lives of people such as David and Rebekah showed clearly that the secret to promotion in the kingdom is servanthood, I studied Genesis 24 more closely. As a result of that study I discovered the authentic qualities of servanthood. You see, not everyone who appears to serve is a servant. I could dress up in a pilot's uniform, briefcase in hand, and walk through Heathrow airport receiving all the respect that comes with the outward clothing, but the true test is when I sit in the pilot's seat, out of the gaze of the admiring public and passengers. In that place I would have to prove it. The pilot's outfit would make me look good for a while, but my true nature would be revealed and my cover blown when the real test came. Judas looked good for a while, Ananias and Sapphira looked good for a while, but when the real test of servanthood came their cover was blown.

Rebekah shows us that true servanthood is not an act but a lifestyle; it is a quality that needs to be inherent in our nature. To begin with, she showed by watering the camels that **real servanthood has genuine motives**. Rebekah had no idea who the servant was, or what he had come to do. She was not responding to an ad in the local paper: 'Vacancies. Rich, affluent, good-looking man seeks wife. Must have a love of spending money, travelling, being instrumental in bringing God into the world and watering camels.'

She did not know that the gaze was on her for promotion. God is observing you, where you are right now. He is placing servant tests for you to pass in your home, work, relationships and church. Some of you are passing up the greatest opportunities for promotion by refusing to sit servanthood tests.

As I look back over my ministry, I can see that some of the most significant turning points and open doors have been as a result of passing such servanthood tests. Pastor Reinhard Bonnke is one of my heroes. He has been an inspiration and an example of a life given over to the cause of the King and his Kingdom. At one of his conferences in Birmingham, England, I volunteered to be one of his helpers. I made myself available to serve wherever I was needed. I was training as a youth evangelist at the time, so I took a week off to help and support. On the first night I wasn't needed: all the ushers had been assigned, all the car park attendants had been assigned, the sales department had all the personnel they needed to handle the tapes, books and videos that would be in demand. So excitedly I settled down at the back of the hall with fourteen thousand other delegates to enjoy the worship and be inspired by the word.

Just before the meeting began, an announcement bellowed out from the massive PA system: 'Would Ray Bevan please come backstage immediately.' Rather surprised and wondering what they needed me to do, I did as requested. When I arrived backstage they informed me they were short of worship singers and asked if I would help. Very nervously I accepted, sang the songs I knew and smiled through the ones I didn't. One night I was asked to sing a solo. I always carry instrumental backing music with me just in case, so I sang a song called 'The little Child', written by Scott Wesley Brown. I was used to singing before large crowds, but here I was singing in front of fourteen thousand people, just before Reinhard was about to preach. The first verse went well, the chorus also, but at the beginning of the second verse my mind went blank. What do you do? You can't stop the music, you can't run off, you just have to continue singing something. That's what I did. I practically composed a whole new second verse on the spot! Judging by the response, I don't think anyone noticed. The amazing thing for me was that as a result of that one song. God opened doors for me to minister in places I had dreamed of going, and he brought people into my life I'd always wanted to meet. The direction of my ministry took a dramatic turn after that week. God was preparing me for the next season of responsibilities and challenges, but I first had to pass the servanthood test.

A few years later, this time in Portugal, Reinhard was holding a Fire Conference in the city of Lisbon (the same conference but a different time and place). His desire was to fire up the church in Portugal and reap a great harvest. By then God had asked me to start a church in Newport (South Wales) called the King's Church. It was early days, we were only about fifty people, and because I believed in what Reinhard was doing and because of the impact these conferences had had on my life, I set aside a week of my time to serve again, at my own expense, in whatever capacity was needed. Prior to the conference, I had worked with the pre-conference team visiting churches in Portugal, preaching, teaching and encouraging Christians to support the conference and get involved. When the conference started, I was once again asked to assist in the worship team. On the final day, the event was moved from a conference centre to a vast open field, parallel to the beach in Lisbon, for two huge open-air meetings. The afternoon meeting was to be in the form of a concert, and Reinhard would preach the Gospel. The evening was to take a more traditional form, with praise, worship and preaching, then prayer for salvation and healing. Saturday afternoon arrived in brilliant sunshine and thousands were gathered in the open field: it was a truly wonderful sight. Excitement levels were high, expectation levels were even higher, and I was honoured when they asked me to prepare to sing a couple of songs. Just before the concert began, the organiser informed us that he had just received word that Reinhard was struggling with his voice and wanted to save it for the evening service. What came out of the organiser's mouth next made time stand still for a while: 'Ray, would you preach?' I looked out at the crowd, realising the responsibility that was being placed upon me, and as I did the Lord gently whispered, 'You have been faithful with little, I can now trust you with much.' I believe God trusted me with that awesome task, not because I'd passed the Gifting test, not because I'd passed the Theology test, but because I'd passed the Servanthood test.

God knows where you are and when he needs you, he'll find you. When he does, make sure you're serving somewhere. Many people are striving to be used, while God is looking for those who are usable. Many people are waiting for the 'big break', while God is looking for someone who is broken.

As we have seen, Rebekah was chosen because she passed the servanthood test. Look at this amazing verse: *'Then Rebekah and her maids arose, and they rode on the camels and followed the man. So the servant took Rebekah and departed' (Gen. 24:61).* Isn't this wonderful? She rode on the camels into her destiny. The very thing she served was the means to carry her into her destiny. Spiritual promotion comes on the back of servanthood, not on the back of gifting, personality or luck. Watering camels seems a most unlikely test for greatness, and even more unlikely for transport into spiritual promotion. What camels has God asked you to water? What is it in your life that looks unspectacular and insignificant in terms of ministry in the kingdom? Teaching a Sunday School class, being a mum, shaking hands on the church door, cleaning the toilets? Before I finish this chapter, I want to share with you a wonderful story called *The Red Rose* by Max Lucado and I know you will get the picture.

John Blanchard stood up from the bench, straightened his army uniform and studied the crowd of people making their way through Grand Central Station. He looked for the girl whose heart he knew, but whose face he didn't, the girl with the rose.

His interest in her had begun thirteen months before in a Florida library. Taking a book off the shelf he found himself intrigued, not with the words of the book, but with the notes pencilled in the margin. In the front of the book, he discovered the previous owner's name, Miss Hollis Maynell.

With time and effort, he located her address. She lived in New York City. He wrote her a letter introducing himself and inviting her to correspond. The next day he was shipped overseas for service in World War II. During the next year and one month the two grew to know each other through the mail. Each letter was a seed falling on a fertile heart. A romance was budding.

Blanchard requested a photograph, but she refused. She felt that if he really cared, it wouldn't matter what she looked like.

When the day finally came for him to return from Europe, they scheduled their first meeting – 7.00 pm at the Grand Central in New York. 'You'll recognise me,' she wrote, 'by the red rose I'll be wearing on my lapel.'

So at 7.00 pm he was in the station looking for a girl whose heart he loved, but whose face he'd never seen.

I'll let Mr Blanchard tell you what happened.

A young woman was coming toward me, her figure long and slim. Her blonde hair lay back in curls from her delicate ears; her eyes were as blue as flowers. Her lips and chin had a gentle firmness, and in her pale green suit she was like springtime come alive. I started toward her, entirely forgetting to notice that she was not wearing a rose. As I moved, a small provocative smile turned her lips. 'Going my way, sailor?' she murmured.

Almost uncontrollably I made one step closer to her, and then I saw Hollis Maynell.

She was standing almost directly behind the girl. A woman well past 40, she had greying hair tucked under a worn hat. She was more than plump, her thick-ankled feet thrust into low-heeled shoes. The girl in the green suit was quickly walking away. I felt as though I was split in two. So keen was my desire to follow her, and yet so deep was my longing for the woman whose spirit had truly companioned and upheld mine.

And there she stood. Her pale, plump face was gentle and sensible, her grey eyes had a warm and kindly twinkle. I did not hesitate. My fingers gripped the small worn blue leather copy of the book that was to identify me to her. This would not be love, but it would be something precious, something perhaps even better than love, a friendship for which I had been and must ever be grateful.

I squared my shoulders and saluted and held out the book to the woman, even though while I spoke I felt choked by the bitterness of my disappointment. 'I'm Lieutenant John Blanchard, and you must be Miss Maynell. I am so glad you could meet me; may I take you to dinner?'

*The woman's face broadened into a tolerant smile. 'I don't know what this is about, son,' she answered, 'but the young lady in the green suit who just went by, she begged me to wear this rose on my coat. And she said if you were to ask me out to dinner, I should go and tell you that she is waiting for you in the big restaurant across the street. **She said it was some kind of test!'***

CHAPTER 10

The Submission Test

We have seen that David 'rose early', passing the Passion Test, 'left the sheep with a keeper', passing the Responsibility Test, and 'took the things and went', passing the Servanthood Test. Finally, and very importantly, if you desire to be the leader God has called you to be, you have to pass the **Submission Test:** *'He went as Jesse had commanded him.'*

Before you can be trusted with leadership, you will have to be proven in 'followship'. The Bible says of the early church believers that *'they devoted themselves to the apostles' doctrine, fellowship, breaking bread and prayers.'* They didn't have to be followed up, there were no exhorting phone calls asking, 'Why weren't you at the meeting?' There was an in-built desire to commit, submit and be loyal to local church and leadership.

Recently, while teaching my church the importance of commitment and loyalty to the local church and its leadership, I came across a scripture in *Joshua (1:2)*, where God was giving instructions to Joshua on how to prepare the people to enter the Promised Land and how to lead them successfully. He says to Joshua, *'Moses My servant is dead. Now therefore, arise, go over this Jordan, **you and all this people**, to the land which I am giving to them – the children of Israel.'* Joshua's response could have been, 'Oh no, Lord, I saw what happened to Moses **with all those people** he had to deal with; there was nothing but problems. Wouldn't it be safer, easier, quicker and less hassle if just Caleb and I went?' Whether Joshua liked it or not, there is no such thing as lone Christianity: it's 'You and all these people.' God's plan has not changed: it is still you and all these people. One of the hardest things we are called to do is to be committed to fellowship in the local church. It is the place where we have to pass the submission test. There are many who have experienced abuse, rejection, dis-appointment and hurt in the local church. Some have experienced the trauma of church splits and the pain of division even among family members, yet while we may all have reason to say, **'Let me go alone, not with all these people,'** God says, 'No, with all their imperfections and inconsistencies, my plan for you is still with all these people, so wake up, get on with the programme and submit as I have commanded.'

Many people don't want to hear the truth concerning the local church, and God's plan for us to be part of it, because with understanding comes responsibility. God's prototype is found in *Acts 2:1-4, 41-47*. While reading these verses I noticed something very important that will help us in our understanding of why and how to obey God's command to commit to the local church and submit to its leadership. After Pentecost the first local church was formed. There was no other model to compare it with, no other church to run to if you didn't agree with the leadership or didn't like 'all those people' who attended.

There is a fictional story that illustrates how fickle we are when it comes to committing to the local church. The story tells of a man who, having been abandoned as a child, spent his life on a desert island. He miraculously survived but longed to be rescued and enjoy the company of other people. One day, a cruise liner was passing the remote island, so he attracted their attention by lighting a fire and a rescue party was dispatched from the ship. On arrival they were amazed to find this man, now in his forties, in his right mind and healthy. The captain looked over the man's shoulder and saw three straw huts that he had built. 'I am fascinated by the three huts behind you,' said the captain. 'Who lives in them? I thought you were the only inhabitant on this island.' 'Oh,' said the man, 'the hut on the left is my house, and the one in the middle is the church I attend every Sunday.' 'That's wonderful,' said the captain. 'But who lives in the other hut?' 'Oh,' said the man, 'that's the church I used to go to!' As funny as that sounds, the church, especially in my nation of Wales, has a history of division, simply because we haven't understood the important principle of submission and commitment to the local church and its leadership.

Jesus' plan for you after you have been saved is the local church: *'And the Lord added to the church daily those who were being saved' (Acts 2:47).*

The Lord Jesus himself saved them and then placed them in a local church, not in a house group, in a ministry or attached to a personality, but in the local church. If only we could grasp that the local church is not a man-made idea but something God has instituted and is high on his list of priorities for all those who are saved. Jesus' core purpose, as I see it, is divided into four parts:

1: To please the Father

'My food is to do the will of Him who sent me, and to finish His work' (Jn. 4:34).

'And this is the will of Him who sent Me, that everyone who sees the Son and believes in Him may have everlasting life' (Jn. 6:40).

2: To seek and to save the lost

'The Son of Man has come to seek and save that which was lost' (Lk. 19:10).

3: To destroy the works of the devil

'For this purpose the Son of God was manifested, that He might destroy the works of the devil' (1 Jn. 3:8).

4: To build his church

'I will build my church, and the gates of Hades shall not prevail against it' (Mt. 16:18).

I believe if our core purpose in life lines up with that of Jesus we will prosper. I wonder how we would score on a scale of one to ten on each of these core values of Jesus:

1: To please the Father

Does his Word have final say in your life? Does his Word govern the decisions you make regarding your finances, family, social life and relationships?

2: To seek and to save the lost

Are you actually seeking to influence men and disciple people for the kingdom?

3: To destroy the works of the devil

This relates not just to healing and deliverance, but also to lifestyle. Do we destroy the spirit of lying by speaking the truth? Do we destroy the spirit of hatred by loving? Do we destroy the spirit of deception and dishonesty by integrity, sincerity and transparency?

4: To build his church

Are we only connected to, committed to and submitted to the local church mandate, or are we actually building it? This was one of Jesus' core values and must be ours.

One area where the fear of God sobers me is this last one. By God's grace I don't ever want to be marked as a divisive man concerning the local church. I don't ever want to be a rebel against authority in the church. I don't ever want to be a hindrance to unity in the church, and I don't ever want to be a hindrance to the purpose of the church. Jesus' purpose is to build the church, not divide and destroy it. If we are to walk in a manner that is pleasing to God and know his favour, we must have such core values.

Paul, writing to the Corinthian church, rebuked them for their factions, cliques and divisions, and went on to declare that possibly some had died before their allotted time because they had not discerned the Lord's body. In *1 Corinthians 11* he effectively said, *'Some of you are sick and lack strength because you are seeking to divide the church rather than build it.'*

While our being added to the church is his choice, the responsibility to function in it is ours. Coming to understand that God's plan is for 'you and all those people' may be one of the hardest things you have to do and accept, but God would never ask you to do what he has not empowered you to do. God's heart is the local church, and his Spirit gives us power to do and be what he's called us to do and be.

God wants us to understand that not only are we responsible to be part of the local church but also he has given us the power to function in it. There are two supernatural baptisms after we are saved:

1. A baptism that **places** you into the Body of Christ *(1 Cor. 12:13).*

2. A baptism that **empowers** you to function in the Body of Christ *(Acts 1:8).*

We will all be held responsible for how we steward these baptisms. The baptism that places us in the church deals with our behaviour in it, while the baptism that empowers us deals with our ministry in it. When it comes to commitment and submission to the responsibilities we all have in relation to the local church, we will have no excuse when we stand before God. For not only has he placed us in the church supernaturally, he has also empowered us to function in it supernaturally. He has empowered us to journey with, interact and live with 'all these people'.

Pentecost was more than speaking in other tongues. The power of Pentecost enabled them to be joined to many others in relationship and ministry and gave them the synergy to function as one unit. As I read *Acts 2:1-4, 41-47*, I realised there are ten areas of local church in which God has empowered us to be and to do. Before I mention the areas, there is something else I noticed in *Acts 2:2: 'And suddenly there came a sound from heaven, as of a rushing mighty wind,* **and it filled the whole house where they were sitting.**' The one thing that grabbed me about this supernatural event in Acts 2 was not the wind, the tongues of fire or the speaking in tongues; it was the posture of the people. They were 'sitting'. Sitting implies rest, peace, acceptance and permanence. It doesn't say the Holy Spirit filled those who were running, jumping or walking; the power was for those who were sitting. When you find a local church where you can sit, where you find rest, peace, acceptance and permanence, there is power available to enable you to be all God has called you to be. **God does not waste power on jumpers, runners and walkers; such power is reserved and targeted for sitters.**

They were not standing up on their way out saying, 'Well, there's nothing happening here, it's a waste of time, we've been here long enough, I'm off.' They were not pacing agitatedly because they were irritated with 'all these people'. 'When Jesus told me to come to the Upper Room, he didn't tell me he would be here or she would be here. These people just irritate me: I'm off.' No, those people on the day of Pentecost, waiting in an upper room, were sitting. They had made up their minds to wait, no matter how long, because that is where God had told them to be. It is very important that you find a place where you can sit. Some of you may have been to churches in the past few years where you can't settle, you get easily offended, you find fault, you don't get your way, you don't like the music: the list is endless. If you don't get a revelation that the power of Pentecost is for those who are sitting, you will never enjoy what God really has for you. Find a local church, make a decision to sit with 'all these people' and you'll be amazed to find your Christian life will go to a new level.

I know there are areas of local church life that are very difficult to embrace. Perhaps that's the reason why you are continuously on the move. It may be you find it difficult to relate to people in small groups because of your personality, or to submit to leadership because of a bad experience. Whatever the reason, there is no excuse for anyone to say, 'I can't sit in a local church', because we have been empowered to behave the way God expects. We can do and be all things through Christ.

As we look at each of the ten areas, if there is one area you find difficulty with, by faith, believe for God to help you. Whichever area you find difficult, God encourages you to reach inside and tap into his power to overcome your fears, inadequacies, stubbornness and pride. Here are the ten areas of empowerment. We have been empowered to:

1   Lead *(Acts 2:14)*

2   Follow *(Acts 2:41-42)*

3   Relate *(Acts 2:42, 46)*

4   Pray *(Acts 2:42)*

5   Commit *(Acts 2:42-46)*

6   Demonstrate *(Acts 2:43)*

7   Give *(Acts 2:44-45)*

8   Praise *(Acts 2:47)*

9   Influence *(Acts 2:47)*

10   Reach *(Acts 1:8)*

Time and space forbid me to write on all of these areas: that would be a book in itself. But let me finish this chapter by focusing on two: the power to lead and the power to relate. The one is closely connected to the other. There is so much leadership potential wasted because people are afraid to, or refuse to, be rooted in the local church.

The first ten years of my Christian life were spent serving in a small Pentecostal church in South Wales. Sometimes it was boring, sometimes I didn't like the people, sometimes I was offended. I had plenty of opportunity to run and go somewhere else, but I realised that if I did, it would only be a matter of time before these things happened in the next church. So I stuck with it, taught in Sunday School, served when asked, went to the Sunday services, went to the Tuesday night prayer meeting, the Thursday night Bible study, the special celebrations and the early morning prayer meetings. I didn't know it at the time, but God was building local church backbone into me and creating opportunity to develop my leadership skills. There are great leaders reading these words: you don't know it yet, but God is preparing you and raising you up to be an effective leader. It doesn't look like it or feel like it yet, especially for a local church member committed to the routine of commitment, living in the mundane rather than the miraculous. Right where you are, with the people God has ordered you to be with, is the best place for you to discover your leadership ability. Look at Peter's example in *Acts 2:14: 'But Peter, standing up with the eleven, raised his voice and said to them…'* Pentecost needed an explanation; the confused multitude needed a leader to speak. What amazes me is that out of all the people in the Upper Room that day, it was Peter who filled the spot. Fifty days earlier he had been a blaspheming, backslidden failure. If someone had told Peter fifty days earlier he would be used as the key leader to plant the first local church of the New Testament and influence thousands by word and deed, he would have laughed at them; but because he was found 'sitting with all those people' he received empowerment to defeat the giants of inadequacy, inferiority, self-doubt and a disastrous failure record and take his place as one of the pillars of the early church.

There is so much said in the statements **'He stood up'**, **'With the eleven',** and **'Raised his voice'**. The simple keys to Peter releasing his leadership potential are found in these words: **'He stood up'** – **'He got restored'; 'With the eleven'** – 'He got related'; **'Raised his voice'** – **'He got responsible'**.

The first thing Peter had to do was stand up. In his case, he needed to get restored from the crippling guilt of failure. You cannot stand up with baggage, whether it be the baggage of regret, unforgiveness or remorse. We have to lay aside 'every weight'. Your leadership potential will not be released until you stand up. It is interesting to discover where Peter's leadership qualities were discovered, recognised, developed and supported: *'Peter stood up with the eleven.'* The leaders God is raising up are not loners, they are not isolated or independent egotists trying to 'make it' in the ministry; they are people who stand up with others. The others who stood up with him knew him well. They knew the good, the bad and the ugly about Peter, but recognised the call and grace of God in his life. The reason why a man may not stay in a local church for long is because he doesn't want people to find out what he is really like. Such people want to be put on a pedestal and be untouchable. They live in an 'image bubble' and when people come too close they are afraid the bubble will burst and people will realise there is an imperfect person inside. The sad thing is that those looking in all know it. The only one who doesn't is the person in the bubble. Many high-profile leaders have become like Hollywood stars: untouchable, unrealistic and unbelievable. They still haven't realised the treasure is in an earthen vessel.

Remember the parable that Jesus told of a man who bought a whole field just to get the treasure buried within it? That is what God did for us. He owns the treasure and the dirt. Remember when Jesus spat on the ground and mixed the spit and the dirt and placed it on a blind man's eyes and healed him? Well, nothing has changed. To heal a hurting world he takes his divine spirit, mixes it with our earthly clay and makes a healing solution for our broken world.

If someone comes up to you and says, 'Don't they know who you think you are?' you have got a problem. *'Peter stood up with the eleven'*. He related. The best place to discover, recognise, develop and find support for your leadership qualities is in the local church. Before Peter was found standing with the eleven as a leader, he was found sitting with them in honest, open relationships. Not only was Peter sitting with the one hundred and twenty in celebration, he was relating to eleven in a small group.

For years my experience of church was only fifty per cent of what it should have been: Sunday morning, Sunday night, Tuesday night, Thursday night. I met people but never related to them. I met people at celebration meetings, had a ten-minute chat after the service, but there was no real relationship, accountability or interaction. To be honest, it suited me because I dreaded the very thought of small groups. You may feel the same way; in a small group you feel vulnerable, exposed and embarrassed. You prefer the big meetings where you can just sit in your own little world, like an egg in a carton. You are sitting in the same carton but your shell protects you. What you don't realise is that the shell you think is protecting you is actually preventing you. It prevents you releasing your life-giving potential with all the other eggs, allowing God to whisk you together to make something that will feed the world. To be the leader God wants you to be, you have to sit with the eleven in relationship before they will stand with you in leadership.

Bill Hybels says in his book *Courageous Leadership*: *'Local church is the hope of the world and its future rests primarily in the hands of its leaders.'* It is time for 'Peters' everywhere, the most unlikely and unusable, to stand up with the eleven and raise their voice. The world is looking for and waiting for local church-grown, authentic leadership that has passed the submission test.

CHAPTER 11

The Wisdom Test

So far, as we have studied God's process of development in David's life that prepared him for one of the most famous victories in the Bible, we have discovered that in order for him to be found ready for the Master's hand, he had to be patient in his calling and faithful in his father's house. In this part of his preparation, we find that he was wise concerning the battle. Thus he was patient and faithful, but also wise.

One thing that impresses me about David as he arrives on the scene is that not only does he not fear Goliath, but also his focus on Goliath is resolute. Although the job he had to do may have been unknown to him (at that stage), he had been prepared for it. He rose to the challenge and stunned both nations with his faith and courage.

As you read these words, you may be about to step into a situation that has been predestined by God: it is what you have been prepared for. If you are to rise up and fulfil your assignment, one thing is absolutely necessary to ensure success. It is not necessarily gifting, authority or revelation, for the main ingredient in David's armoury that enabled him to take Goliath out was focus. Every great man and woman of God who has done anything for him has had this quality. Paul's classic statement speaks for them all in *Philippians 3:12-15: 'One thing I do'* – my heart and mind are focused, I live for one thing, I eat it, sleep it and live it. It is so important. All my energy, emotional spirit and mental power are channelled into it.

The call of God on my life and what he has called me to do is life or death to me, 'I reach for it', 'press forward'. Forget the past. This is the reason I discipline myself, choose my friends and sacrifice anything else. Paul exhorts us to 'have this mindset' *(Phil. 3:15)*, to stay focused on the task given us. Jesus 'set his face as a flint' toward his purpose; he only did those things that pleased the Father. *'The spirit of the Lord is upon me because...'* Jesus knew the reason for the anointing: it was not so he could become a world-famous evangelist, nor was it so he could experience spiritual manifestations or have new feelings and experiences. The anointing was given for a purpose: to heal, deliver and declare. He knew it and he stayed focused to complete it.

The biggest temptation we have as we seek to finish our course is not demonic power or a difficult assignment: it is distraction. When David turned up, cheese sandwiches in hand, surveying the scene, an arrogant uncircumcised Philistine defying what should have been a bold, confident, covenant-minded army, everything within him cried out, **'Something needs to be done about this.'**

Is that where you are right now? You have stepped into a situation that has drawn out the same response from your heart. Every great leader that has left their mark in history started here. In 1789 William

Wilberforce stood before Parliament and passionately and eloquently cried out for the day when men, women and children would no longer be bought and sold in open markets like farm animals. Each year for eighteen years he remained focused, and each year for eighteen years his bill was defeated. The cry in his heart grew louder: **'Something needs to be done about this.'** It kept him focused until in 1833, four days before his death: he went to be with God knowing Parliament had finally bowed the knee to his consistent, passionate, focused mission and passed a bill abolishing slavery from our shores.

Who can forget Martin Luther King standing on the steps of the Lincoln Memorial and with his words painting a picture of a world without prejudice, hatred or racism? 'I have a dream that my four children will one day live in a nation where they will not be judged by the colour of their skin but by the content of their character.' **Something had to be done**. It moved this man to a totally focused passion that resulted in radical changes concerning racism around the world. Although he was assassinated for it, his dream lives on and history records his victory as he stood before his Goliath, focused.

The power of vision, the power of a focused mind, constructing rails for the locomotive. A target for the arrow is what is needed for you to be successful in your calling. Remove the goal posts from the soccer pitch and you reduce the game to twenty-two men having ninety minutes of exercise. Remove the holes on a golf course and the game would be reduced to a scenic walk. Remove vision from a leader and you cut out his heart.

Winston Churchill has gone down in history as one of the greatest leaders of the twentieth century. His rise to prominence came as a result of that cry. As a Chaplin-moustached tyrant rose up from the ranks of Germany and began to spread his tentacles of horror across Europe, Churchill stood up before the British people and declared, 'We are resolved to destroy Hitler and every vestige of the Nazi regime.

From this, nothing will turn us. Nothing! We will never parley. We will never negotiate with Hitler or any of his gang. We shall fight him by land. We shall fight him by sea. We shall fight him in the air. Until, with God's help, we have rid the earth of his shadow.' Wonderful stuff. As Churchill, along with the world, watched this global threat to democracy, the cry rose up in his heart, **'Something has to be done,'** and he remained focused until it became a reality.

What stirs your heart? What arouses your righteous anger? What is it in your life that causes this cry to explode within you: **'Something needs to be done'**? Is it the crime rate in your city, the lack of workers in your church, the lack of personal growth in your life? Apathy is the sleeping sickness that kills potential and stops change. David cried out in the face of cowardice, apathy and fear and said, 'For who is this uncircumcised Philistine, that he should defy the armies of the living God?' David threw down his cheese sandwiches as that cry within him became deafening. A cry that rose above the cries of fear from the armies of Israel, a cry that rose above the battle cry of the enemy, a cry that rose above his own sense of inadequacy and inferiority. But along with the stirrings of passion there must also be the steel of focus.

David was surrounded by voices of distraction; he was bombarded from all sides by spiritual 'suckers' that threatened to divert the sap of vision into unproductive battle. David did not waste time fighting the wrong giant. The five smooth stones were not wasted on the wrong target. In fact, I noticed that there were five giants he could have been distracted to fight, but he resisted the power of their attraction and stayed focused:

First, there was the giant of 'family familiarity'. We see from *1 Samuel 17:28-30* that those who should have been there to encourage and help him were the very ones who opposed him. Inferiority can easily breed in this environment: don't be bullied by it. Don't stop to fight the giant of family familiarity, whether natural or spiritual. The giant of family familiarity wants to hold you to your past and prevent you moving ahead. Jesus was confronted by such a giant, one who tried to distract him from the purpose of his birth *(Mt. 13:54-58)*. The people who grew up with him, who knew him 'back then', did not have the ability to know him now. They assessed his potential on the basis of their perspective of his past. He was hindered because of their limited vision. They were more familiar with his past than with his present. David, at the point of crisis concerning the battle, was tempted to be distracted into responding to his brothers' accusations and criticisms: 'We know you, David, we were raised with you. You're the family runt. You're the sheep-keeper, blah blah blah.' Perhaps you are being held back by the 'I knew you when...' crowd. They keep you stuck in a stage of your life that is past and gone. These people, whether they be family, friends or associates, define you on the basis of who you were, not who you have become and certainly not who you can someday become. You can't afford to allow those close to you, whether in your natural or spiritual family, to use words that cause the bully of inferiority to step into that area of your life and keep you paralysed. Inferiority is a bully that feeds on the food provided by family familiarity. It's time to stand up and say, 'I'm not being bullied any more.' Don't waste any more time being distracted by this bully. Your real giant is waiting to be knocked out. The bully of inferiority rises up and intimidates us every time we want to go to the next level with God.

The Bible says of a man, 'As he thinks in his heart, so he is.' Studies have shown that our thinking controls our behaviour. Not just affects our behaviour, but controls it. If your parents told you were worthless, you will live like that until the pattern is broken. If circumstances have told you you'll never make it, you will live like that until the pattern is broken. The dangers of giving in to the bully are many. Here are three:

Conformity: Inferiority stifles personal opinion and individuality, because you lack the confidence to be different.

Immobility: You feel worthless, so you do nothing. You're afraid to get involved. The children of Israel were stirred into mobility because of this bully: 'We seemed like grasshoppers in our own eyes and we looked the same to them.' As a result they allowed this bully to dictate the terms. They wandered around for a lifetime, living a second-class life, never enjoying God's best. The scene David witnessed was the same. There was a more dangerous bully that paralysed the armies of Israel that day. It wasn't the giant in the enemy camp, it was one in his own. It wasn't the giant shouting defiantly in the valley of Elah that immobilised them, it was the bully standing in their hearts.

Inferiority: David was focused and did not allow family familiarity to feed the bullies in his life. He knew Goliath was not going to win that day. David did not act rebelliously toward his brothers; he didn't react defensively with abuse or self-justification. He just stopped, focused and prepared to take Goliath out. You and I must do the same.

A few years ago I was ministering at the annual celebration conference at the church pastored by Ray McCauley (Rhema, Johannesburg) and sharing ministry with a very powerful preacher, T.D. Jakes. If I describe him as a very powerful preacher, I know what I'm talking about: I had to speak in the meeting after he spoke! He preached a wonderful sermon from Romans 8, from which I received personal help and fresh revelation. He taught us to start praying the 'I don't know' prayer. At the time, I was in the middle of the biggest personal battle I had ever fought. I was confused, vulnerable, hurt, afraid, and really didn't know how to deal with the many voices that were shouting at me, demanding answers. I started to pray the 'I don't know' prayer and my whole life began to start rearranging. God started moving the furniture until I didn't recognise the landscape any more.

Let me try to communicate what he taught me that day. In *Romans 8:22* Paul writes, *'We know'*. In verse 28 of the same chapter, he writes, *'We know'*, but in verse 26 he writes, *'We do not know.'* Paul was knowledgeable in areas of God's sovereignty and love, but when it came to personal specifics, personal decisions regarding places, people and plans, there were times when he just didn't know. That's the time he had full dependence on the Holy Spirit to help him. What a relief it was for me to hear Pastor Jakes declare from the Bible that it's OK to stand up and say sometimes, 'I don't know.' That's where I was. I didn't know whom I could trust, even when it came to my own personal matters and decisions. I was unsure and I needed help.

The 'I don't know' prayer came in four parts, but I have to tell you that this prayer comes with a life warning. If you pray it and mean it, it could rearrange your life for ever. Here it is:

1. Take out of my life the people I don't need. Bring into my life the people I do need, because I don't know who is who.

2. Don't give me anything I can't handle, because I don't know when to say 'Yes' or when to say 'No'.

3. Open the doors I need to walk through and close the doors I do not need to walk through, because I don't know which is which.

4. Help me to understand the seasons of my life, because I don't know how to distinguish them.

This is a prayer of relinquishment, where you give God the fine details of your life. If that's where you are right now, at a crossroads in your life, surrounded by many confusing voices, feelings and circumstances, stand still, pray this prayer and be prepared for some surprises. Like David, you are tempted to waste time and energy on people who through familiarity are shackling you with their negative words, who demand you turn away from God and from every assignment and believe what they say about you. Don't do it: you're fighting the wrong giant. Pray the 'I don't know' prayer and trust God for the outcome. In the next chapter, as we talk about another giant that David refused to waste his time fighting, I will be sharing with you some of the most important lessons I have learned in the ministry. Refuse to fight the giant of other people's opinions.

CHAPTER 12

The Giant of Other People's Opinions

'Why did you come down here? And with whom did you leave the sheep? We know your pride and the insolence of your heart': these were the words that greeted David when all he had come to do was to serve his brothers at the request of their father – a barrage of accusation directed at the very core of David's being. The verbal missile assault was aimed at the very foundation of his character. David, we know you. We know why you do things: your motives are wrong, you have a hidden agenda; come clean, tell us why you're really here.

If David had been insecure or had allowed his mind to meditate on this verbal venom, perhaps doubt would have crept into his heart and caused him to ask himself certain questions. 'Am I really like that? They are my brothers, they know me; am I arrogant, am I insolent, am

I irresponsible?' David did not waste his time fighting the giant of other people's opinions, and neither should you. Do not let people's opinions of you be judge and jury in your heart. Take your heart to God, for he is the only one who knows.

Perhaps the brothers judged David with the same judgement they would use on themselves. Perhaps Eliab was still offended by the selection criteria of Samuel: *'So it was, when they came, that he looked at Eliab* and said, *"surely the Lord's anointed is before Him!"* But the Lord said to Samuel, *"Do not look at his appearance or at his physical stature, because I have refused him. For the Lord does not see as man sees; for man looks at the outward appearance, but the Lord looks at the heart"'* (1 Sam. 16:6-7). **David was chosen because of the purity of his heart, and so it was to that area that the attack came.** David was unmoved by the challenge. He replied, 'What have I done now?' implying that this was not the first time Eliab had verbally attacked him. 'Is there not a cause?' The one thing that helped David to stay immune to these spiritual heart attacks was 'the cause.' The cause that day was the death of Goliath. He refused to get involved in a battle with the wrong giant. Whatever people thought of him, whatever their opinion of him, nothing was going to sidetrack him from his cause. Your destiny and calling are unique. Only you can run your race, only you can finish your course. You're not perfect; you will make mistakes. Your motives will be questioned and your actions misunderstood. The only way to deal with these attacks and stay focused on your course is to **stay on the cross.**

What do I mean when I say, **'Stay on the cross?'** These were the words the Holy Spirit spoke to me when I was going through the greatest personal trial of my life. Sadly, after twenty-six years of marriage, I found myself in the middle of a very public divorce. Without going into the details, it is enough to say there were no other people involved: the marriage broke down and ended up with my now ex-wife filing for a divorce that became final in October 1998. At the time of that divorce, both the King's Church and I had a very high profile in the community, nationally and internationally. My circumstances became a breeding ground for betrayal, hidden agendas, lies, pointing fingers and wagging tongues. Divorce is a sin and should be treated as such, and in no way do I seek to justify it in this book. But I do thank God there is life after divorce because its not the unpardonable sin. I thought my life was over, my ministry finished, but worst of all to live with was the personal sense of failure, disappointment and shame. People's opinions were erected like gallows, demanding that I put the noose around my neck and hang. But something deep inside cried out to a God of mercy, who replied with these words: **'Don't be moved by what people say or think; rejoice because of what heaven knows.'** As far as I knew, I had opened my heart before God, asking his forgiveness and cleansing for any motive that would have caused unrighteous behaviour. I cried out to the Righteous Judge, as had David before me, *'Create in me a clean heart, O God, and renew a right spirit within me. Do not cast me away from your presence and do not take your Holy Spirit from me. Restore to me the joy of your salvation and uphold me by your generous spirit, then I will lead transgressors to your ways and sinners shall be converted to you.'*

In the midst of people's opinions that threatened to crush my life, I submitted the core of my being to God. When I even doubted my own motives, I relinquished all judgement to him. Don't put flowers on anyone's grave until they are dead. Don't write anyone off because of opinion based on surface or second-hand information. The mercy of God qualifies the disqualified. The mercy of God annuls law. The mercy of God dissolves judgement. My divorce was not the plan of God, but I have learned more intensely that God is ultimately a redeemer.

Grace is God's ability to give us what we don't deserve, while mercy is God's ability to restrain from giving us what we do deserve. The church in Europe needs a fresh revelation of the mercy of God, especially her leaders. It is the key to reaching, touching and healing a broken world. Jesus has blessed us with ministers of music, helping us to enjoy his presence through praise and worship. He has blessed us with ministers of miracles, raising our expectation level for the release of the supernatural power of God. He has blessed us with ministers of money, teaching us biblical economics, so that we can be blessed financially and be a blessing to others. He has blessed us with ministers of masses, inspiring us to focus on the fields that are white unto harvest. He has blessed us with ministers of movements, men and women who have been catalysts bringing waves of particular anointing, refreshing, releasing and regimenting. I believe in these last days we are going to receive from the risen Christ a blessing of ministers whose strength and anointing will be seeded in their weakness and disqualification. People who feel disqualified because of failure, pain, loss or catastrophe are going to be raised up and given to the Body of Christ as ministers of mercy. God will mercifully take their failure and turn it into fuel. He'll take their loss and turn it into life, take their pain and turn it into passion, and miraculously, turn their catastrophe into a means of comfort and restoration for many. God, through his mercy, will use the dead places of their lives, which seemingly disqualified them from service, as places to cultivate honey. As Samson reached inside the carcass of the dead lion, finding honey to feed and sustain him, so God will do with his ministers of mercy. Untouchables, walking and talking with a transparency that borders on embarrassment; an honesty that dissolves pretentious masks, and warmth that is as irresistible as sunshine to the flower. Through these wounded healers the power of God's comfort will flow and release a river of mercy into this broken world. **Jesus' wounds were used positively, healing, saving and delivering. Begin to see your wounds as having the same potential.**

As you read this, you may be wasting your present by regretting a wasted past. You may feel disqualified because of failure, pain, loss or catastrophe. Be encouraged: what the devil has been using to cause a stink in your life, God will use as fertiliser to produce new growth. If it weren't for mercy, God would have to return incarnate and evangelise the world himself, because without mercy he would find no material to work with. Just the other day, I was wondering what the biggest botch-up of all time would have been. Without hesitation, Adam and Eve's mess-up came to mind, and with it the realisation that my own past mess-ups didn't even come close. God could have walked into that mess in a number of ways. He could have walked in as Executioner. 'Adam and Eve, you've messed up, you've been tried, found guilty and sentenced; goodbye!' He could have walked in as Creator, and started all over again. He did neither, even though he had the reason and the power to do so. No! He walked into that mess as Redeemer. There is no catastrophe, failure, pain or loss that God cannot redeem and use for good; because mercy does not give us what we deserve; it redeems and restores. As we have seen, mercy qualifies the disqualified, it annuls law and dissolves judgement, for *'in judgement God does not remember what we deserve, he remembers mercy'*. **The law stops every mouth and leaves you speechless. Mercy covers every sin and leaves you breathless.**

My wife Laila is Norwegian by birth, and on a recent visit to Norway she introduced me to the valleys, rivers and mountains that were her companions for the first sixteen years of her life. Kjellstadli, tucked away in the splintered coastline of the West, was the base from where we visited spectacular fjords, amazing ice formations, majestic mountains and gorgeous valleys. Whenever I was asked, 'What do you think of that?' the only two words that came out of my mouth were, 'Wow! Wow!' The whole experience left me breathless. Mercy is like that. As God takes you by the Holy Spirit on a trip through his story, worked out in ordinary people as seen in Scripture, as he shows you his mercy, the incredible ingredient that enables him to use murderers, womanisers, cheats and racists, to administer his will, you will be left breathless. All you can say is, 'Wow!'

Law points to God's standard, and we say, 'How?' Mercy points to his blood and we say, 'Wow!' When we see Jesus sitting by a well and asking a Samaritan woman for a drink, we see mercy at its best. A Jewish Rabbi and a Samaritan whore were not the basis for a meaningful conversation. Before she could receive what he wanted to give her, something had to change: her mindset. As long as she believed the man waiting for her at the well was her worst enemy, she wouldn't expect or receive anything. A vast proportion of the Body of Christ sits by the same well, facing a New Testament situation with Old Testament eyes. The words Jesus spoke to that woman, a woman who had been disqualified by her friends, disqualified by the disciples and probably disqualified by herself, are words you may need to hear right now: *'If you knew the gift of God, and who it is who says to you, "Give me a drink," you would have asked him, and he would have given you living water.'* The key to her asking and receiving was a change in her perception: *'If you only knew*, you would have asked and I would have given.' Jesus was basically saying to this woman, 'You are not going to ask me for anything believing I'm your worst enemy. Understand: judgement doesn't stand before you, mercy does.' Mercy has been waiting for you at this well. Mercy desires to speak with you. Mercy wants to give you a new start. Mercy wants to use you as a minister of mercy to your own city. She got the message and was used by Jesus as the first mass evangelist in the New Testament.

What about you? Do you see God as your worst enemy? You know about his judgement. The New Testament Pharisees have meticulously reminded you of what the law says. You're disqualified, you've failed, you've messed up and your situation is beyond hope. Listen to your Saviour: *'If you only knew.'* It's not a judge sitting at the well, it's not a Pharisee, it's not an executioner, but a minister of mercy, desiring to make you one too.

God has recently given me a fresh mandate to minister mercy to the disqualified. Having gone through a divorce as a minister, and dealing with the rejection, guilt, shame and fear that accompanies such a failure, I pray that this book will be to you as the honey was to Samson. God specifically told me to minister:

1. Hope to fallen trees – *Job 14:8 (Living Bible)*

2. Restoration to burnt stones – *Nehemiah 4:1-3*

3. Strength for bruised reeds – *Isaiah 42:3*

4. Encouragement for dying flames – *Isaiah 42:3 (Living Bible)*

Are you a fallen tree, down and useless because of failure? Are you a burnt stone, burnt and useless because of rejection and disappointment? Are you a smouldering wick, passionless and useless because of despair and hopelessness? Are you a broken reed, demoralised and useless? Jesus wants you to know it is his grace that teaches us to say no to ungodly things. It's his goodness that follows us all the days of our lives and it is his mercy that draws us to come before his throne. In Hebrews 4:16 we see that mercy qualifies the disqualified – come and receive your diploma.

You may be surrounded by people's opinions, which, like the 'Hound of the Baskervilles', are ready to rip you apart. You have a choice whether you allow that or not. You may not have control over what is being said, but you do have a choice over how you respond. When you have a real revelation of mercy, and know that you have committed your case to God, allowed his eyes to gaze into your heart and responded in true humility, you shouldn't care what people think and should rejoice that heaven knows. My advice to you, if you are there, is expressed in the words God spoke to me: 'Stay on the cross: it is safer there.'

Jesus' authenticity, as seen through the eyes of a Roman centurion, did not come through the performing of miracles, the depth of his teaching or even the applause of the crowd that followed him. As the hardened Roman guard looked up at this man, hands and feet skewered to a crude execution post and surrounded by a jeering mob, as he observed the way Jesus conducted himself in the face of the worst circumstances, as he listened to gracious, kind words flow out of his mouth, he was convinced this man was who he said he was. *'Surely this is the Son of God,'* he was reported to have said. The same is true today. People are not looking for perfection but authenticity. People are not looking for the Word made flash, but made flesh. We will win the world not by protecting our image, but by nailing it to a cross and allowing God to display his.

His image is displayed not when people speak well of you but in the way you react when they don't. His image is displayed not when there is an absence of pain, fear or rejection, but in the way you respond to these things. **His image is displayed not when you receive Palm Sunday praise, but in the way you react to Good Friday nails.** During the awful season of my divorce, when I wanted to fight all the accusations of my enemies and justify every motive, the scene portrayed in *Matthew 27:27-50* ruled my vision. I clearly heard the Holy Spirit say to me, 'Stay on the cross, it is safer there.'

Jesus taught me three of the most important lessons I could learn and pass on to others, concerning what to do when you are tempted to fight the giant of people's opinions.

Firstly: Stay on the cross when you are tempted to get revenge on your enemies

Matthew 27:41-43 shows us that his enemies surrounded him like a pack of wolves, gloating over what they thought was his destruction and sickly taunting him to come off the cross and prove himself to be true. But Jesus knew how to complete his course; he had to walk in forgiveness and stay focused. Are you tempted to seek revenge on your enemies? Are you being falsely accused? Do you find yourself running around trying to answer every critic who shouts from the crowd? Do you feel your hands are nailed, so you can't do anything to prove you are right? Are your feet immobilised, so there's no place to walk and hide? Is your need to be heard drowned out by the gloating, jeering comments and opinions of others? In your heart, do you secretly want their destruction? If you have submitted your case to the Father, you have nothing to fear. He is in complete control. But you say, 'If I just hang here and forgive them, doesn't that give their deeds credibility?' No! Forgiveness doesn't make them right – it keeps you free. Free to praise your God. Free to make godly choices. Free to fly above the low level of the mob. Stay on the cross: it's safer there.

Secondly: Stay on the cross when you are tempted to interfere on behalf of those you love

From the cross, Jesus saw the pain and wonder in his mother's eyes. Don't you think he wanted to come off the cross to provide protection and answers to those people who had put their trust in him? During the most intensely dark days of my marital break-up my experience was that I felt exposed as a pastor, vulnerable and helpless; but the worst part of all was to look into the eyes of those who had put their trust in me and not be able to give them the details of what I was going through. I kept the congregation informed of general developments and I had great help from men of God around the world, but at the end of the day, I felt so alone and so hurt as I watched the flock begin to scatter. There may be a pastor reading these words, and for whatever reason, you are in the same situation. Those who look up to you are longing for some detailed explanation of what's happening and all you can say to them is, 'Trust God and love me.' God will work it all out. It is amazing how God can take even our mistakes and our failures, mix them with our repentant heart and his mercy and adapt it to his will, and produce something even better.

The mercy of God is every Pharisee's nightmare. It enables him to forgive a murderer and adulterer and allow him to go back to the very woman with whom he committed the crime and produce a Solomon, from whose line the Saviour of the world came. As Philip Yancey says in his book *What's So Amazing About Grace? 'Grace doesn't add up, grace isn't fair.'* As I watched people leave the church, some for theological reasons, some because they just didn't know who to believe (some were gullible victims of rumour and gossip), some because they simply saw it as an opportunity to leave anyway, I wanted to shout from where I was, 'Don't leave, trust me. I can't tell you everything now but eventually truth and time will clear the fog.' But it seemed there was a divine process in operation, one with which I was unfamiliar. It felt as though I was in a state of metamorphosis; I was moving from one season to another and all I could do was obey his command: 'Stay on the cross and watch.' When I prayed the 'I don't know' prayer and obeyed his word to stay on the cross, the church experienced what I now know to be a process of winnowing. All I know is that during the season of winnowing, the safest place for any pastor, leader and Christian to be is on the cross, allowing God to do what he wants to do.

Luke 3:17 talks about God holding the winnowing fork in his hand. We understand the agricultural principle of sowing and reaping, of seedtime and harvest. Laws placed into existence by God work positively and negatively, naturally and spiritually. I was familiar with such principles, but winnowing was something that was new to me. Let me give you a basic understanding of the principle of winnowing. It will help you in a difficult climate and during a season of relationship crisis and wondering. A farmer brings in the harvest, takes the main crop for sale or manufacture and takes a small part of the harvest to winnow, to produce seed for the next harvest. With the winnowing fork in his hand, he throws the corn into the air against the wind. The wind blows out the chaff and debris, allowing the seed to fall to the ground, cleansed of what is not needed for the next harvest. He then takes the corn that has been winnowed and places it in a barn to be stored ready to plant for the next season. Everything he needs for his next season is contained in these winnowed seeds. When moving us from one season to the next, God sometimes winnows. It is the same as with the corn. He throws us up; he throws our churches up against the breath of his mouth and blows out what will not beautify us for the next season of our lives. It could be people, habits or things. It's uncomfortable, scary, humbling, but it's necessary if you are to go on to the next season.

David understood this principle of winnowing. In *Psalm 139:3* he says, *'You comprehend my path and my lying down.'* The literal meaning of the word used for 'comprehend' is 'winnow'. 'You throw my destiny, my way forward, up against your breath and you winnow, blowing away what could be a hindrance for the next season of my life.' You may watch helplessly from a cross as people distrust you, leave and forsake you. If God is winnowing people out of your life, don't run after them. It doesn't mean the people who leave you are right or wrong, good or bad. It just means they are not meant to be part of the seed for the next season of your life. You may not know it yet, but where you are going they can't go. God has other plans for them. Is God winnowing people out of your life? Is God winnowing things out of your life? If so, stand still. Stay on the cross. He is storing seed for the next season of your life.

Thirdly: Stay on the cross when you are tempted to protect your reputation.

This was the most powerful lesson I learned. We pray religiously, 'Lord, I want to be like you' until it touches our reputation. I didn't realise how much my reputation meant to me until I lost it. Here I was, pastoring a large, high-profile church in Wales, travelling all over the world, holding conferences that attracted large crowds, enjoying and relishing the prestige and respect from other ministers, and then Bam! This mental hurricane ripped up the very foundation of my heart and branded me a failure. Slowly, over the months leading up to my divorce and beyond, in my own eyes I felt my reputation being eaten away like a cancer. Very often we miss the opportunity to move into the next season because we have too much to lose. If you are seeking to live the cross life, then self-preservation has to be nailed to it.

Why did Judas betray Jesus? Self-preservation.

Why did Peter deny Jesus? Self-preservation.

Why do people betray anybody? Self-preservation.

During times of crisis, God is seeking to expose whether you are living to protect your image or dying to give your reputation away. Philippians 2 declares that Jesus made himself of no reputation. During your Christian life be prepared to have your reputation attacked. For a season on the cross Jesus lost his reputation, but even when under extreme pressure to save it, he stayed on the cross.

His reputation as Truth-stater was lost for a season.

His reputation as Way-maker was lost for a season.

His reputation as Life-giver was lost for a season.

You see, when you are under pressure to keep your reputation, you will find out, as I did, that the root of betrayal is the protection of self-image. The root of denial is the protection of self-image. The root of forsaking a friend is the protection of self-image. You know when you have an image or reputation, because you are prepared to protect the one and lose the other. An image-based mentality will fight to protect self. A reputation-based mentality will die to save others. People with a reputation will die for the bigger picture, even if it means losing it for a season. People with a God-given reputation realise they received it by acts of grace, not by works of the flesh. They are prepared to give it up because they know they didn't produce it. People with an image will betray, run and forsake in order to protect it.

The essence of image is self-preservation. People protecting their image live to please man, not God; to protect themselves, not save others. Run from people who gossip, cause strife, slander or betray, but never run away from a friend who has failed or who is in trouble, because standing with them will affect your image. The Bible says that God holds in high esteem the one *who swears to his own hurt and does not change' (Ps. 15:4)*.

I remember the time when I was reaching out for help and comfort from those I regarded as close friends, only to discover I was branded with the big 'D'. During one conversation one of those friends began to speak to me as if I was about to be buried. His words were like flowers laid at the foot of a grave: 'I remember when you were the darling of the denomination,' he condescendingly whispered. 'I remember when your church had a great image, but now you're divorced, the papers are attacking you, people are saying all manner of things about you,' and as he continued his eulogy, I realised for him it was no longer acceptable to relate to me. The basis for friendship, which I now realised was purely theological, not biblical, had gone. When he finished, I paused and made this statement: 'So, all along you were only a Palm Sunday friend, not a Good Friday friend.' That day I learned something priceless about relationships that will help me for the rest of my life.

I had discovered what true friendship is, and at the same time what it is not. I realised that in many of my relationships, I was living in denial or just plain ignorance. As I sat and thought about those who left my life as a result of my divorce and re-marriage and those who stayed or came in to help, I compiled a list of relationship types. This might help someone, especially those in the ministry, to avoid the hurtful discovery of a misunderstood relationship or a relationship from which your expectation level is a ten when in reality it should only be a two. Here are the relationship types I discovered:

The Ministry Relationship

This relationship is based on a promise: I will relate to you and be your friend because it will help me to grow or advance in my ministry.

The Popularity Relationship

I will relate to you and be your friend as long as you are popular. Your looking good makes me look good.

The Theological Relationship

I will relate to you and be your friend, but if you do something that disagrees with my theology, I'm out.

The Image Relationship

I will relate to you and be your friend, but if what you do or say spoils my image, I'm out.

The Judas Relationship

I will relate to you, but if the going gets tough and I get a better offer, I'm off.

Covenant Relationship

This relationship declares, 'I will relate to you and be your friend whatever happens.' I'm not talking about someone who is your friend and continuously wants to disobey God, live in sin, rejecting all approaches to repent and turn to God; in that case you are actually exhorted not to fellowship or eat with such a person *(1 Cor. 5:9-13)*. I'm talking about sticking with a repentant friend, even if relating to them hurts your reputation. That's why the Pharisees hated Jesus. He was a friend of sinners. God puts a very high value on loyalty in relationships. He expects it in our relationship with him and he expects it in our relationship with others. When Jesus said in *Matthew 5:13*, *'If salt loses its flavour, it is good for nothing but to be trampled underfoot,'* there was a greater depth of meaning than perhaps many of us have understood. After studying the scriptures, I came to see that salt speaks of loyalty in relationships. When God gave instructions on how sacrifices were to be presented to him, he insisted that every sacrifice had to contain salt. In *Leviticus 2:11-13* God explains the offering criteria. I noticed that God forbids two ingredients and demands one. The first ingredient forbidden was leaven. In Scripture, leaven speaks of insincerity, guile and pride. Leaven puffs up bread; leaven makes you appear to be what you are not. Jesus warned people against the *'leaven of the Pharisees'*: they puffed themselves up and appeared to be something they were not. God says, 'Don't come before me and give me something that appears to be, but is not.'

The second ingredient was honey. The effect of honey is to sweeten. In forbidding honey in the sacrifice, God was in fact saying, 'Don't flatter me. Don't try to sweeten me up to gain advantage. Give me honour, not flattery.' 'With all your offerings,' he says, 'you shall offer salt.' In Old Testament times, salt was very scarce. It was a very valuable commodity. Sometimes people were paid for their services in salt. Our word 'salary' is actually derived from the word for salt. We hear phrases like 'He's not worth his salt', meaning 'He's not worth the time invested in him.' In those days salt was involved in making covenant relationships. When two men entered a covenant relationship, it was a serious thing and firmly binding. Many Eastern men during that time would often carry a pouch of salt around their waist to replace salt lost in perspiration because of the hot sun. To establish the ultimate nature of the covenant, they would each reach into their salt pouch and place some into a separate pouch, then shake the bag so the two portions were thoroughly mixed. Only if one of them could now reach into the bag and retrieve his portion of salt, they said, could the covenant be annulled. In those days a man who broke a covenant was considered worthless. Not worth his salt. 'If salt loses its flavour, it is good for nothing but to be trampled underfoot.' Covenant relationships are serious. If you break them, you become unsalty, not worth trusting. It's interesting that in Leonardo da Vinci's famous painting 'The Last Supper', as Jesus and Judas are reaching to dip the bread into the bowl, Judas tips over the salt container. Quite symbolic, in that Jesus said, *'He who dipped his hand with Me in the dish will betray Me' (Mt. 26:23).* The overturned salt was a visible demonstration, revealing a traitor's heart. Timothy tells us that in the last days people will be lovers of themselves, betrayers, traitors, disloyal, covenant-breakers, unsalty. A man who loves himself will betray his brother, if it means it will prosper him.

Through my divorce experience and my disappointment in relationships, disappointment in those who said they would stand with me and didn't, I have made a decision that by the grace of God, if I am to be a friend to someone, I desire to be a salty one.

As I bring this chapter to a close, let me share with you the difference between image-protectors and reputation-givers. *John 18:28-36* gives us a perfect picture of people who were experts at protecting their image – the Pharisees. As Pilate tried to pin the Pharisees down as to their reasons for pressuring him to execute Jesus, all they could come up with was that he was an *'evildoer'*: no specifics, just hazy innuendos embroidered into their description of Jesus as an *'evildoer'*. Clouded, finger-pointing, hazy accusation. People trying to discredit someone to save their own image will always give a partly hazy accusation. 'Well, he is just a bad person. Well, we know things we are not at liberty to tell. We can't put our finger on it but it looks bad to us.' Beware of people who use hazy accusation to destroy someone in order to save face. The Pharisees had an image of self-righteousness that had to be protected. When Pilate pressed them for a specific charge, they shook their heads in disbelief that he would even question their accusation. They were Pharisees: hadn't Pilate heard about their impeccable image? It was almost unimaginable that their image would be questioned, and they shouted out, in essence, 'Don't you realise who we are? If he wasn't guilty, we wouldn't bring the accusation. We are Pharisees, we have an image of respectability, goodness, godliness and holiness; you should believe us, whatever the accusation, because of who we are.' But all they had was an image. The Pharisees had an image to maintain before the people, not a reputation before God. Here is a lesson you must learn if you are to survive the gallows of other people's opinions. Beware of people who use their good image to destroy someone's reputation. Stay clear of them: they are spiritual Pharisees protecting their image. Jesus calls them *'whitewashed graves'*, all shiny on the outside but full of dead men's bones on the inside. Only God knows who is holy, righteous and Christ-like. Image-protectors not only try to bring hazy accusations in order to destroy godly reputations, but they also use others to fire bullets. In *verse 31* Pilate says to them, *'You take Him and judge Him according to your law'*. They said to him, *'It is not lawful for us to put anyone to death.'* In other words, we can't do it but you can do it for us. Don't fall into the trap of firing someone else's bullets. Think for yourself; make your own judgements. Before you accept and believe any accusation, irrespective of who develops it, check it out for yourself; don't be caught firing bullets at someone's reputation because of who they are. It is so dangerous, because at the end of the day you will be held accountable for what you think and say.

See how Jesus answers Pilate *(verse 34)* as he questions him on behalf of the Pharisees, saying, *'Are you speaking for yourself about this, or did others tell this you concerning Me?'* Jesus will always bring you back to what you think. Often friendships are broken, people leave churches or families are divided because people are acting on what others have said. In their hearts they want to stay, in their hearts they want to continue the relationship, but sadly their decision is based on the conviction of others, not their own. Through these words I am encouraging you not to become a Pharisee. *Proverbs 17:9* says, *'He who covers a transgression seeks love, but he who repeats a matter separates friends.' Proverbs 17:17* says, *'A friend loves at all times, and a brother is born for adversity.'*

Reputation doesn't fight for self-preservation; it is prepared to die for the bigger picture. Yes, I was tempted to fight the giant of other people's opinions, but as I obeyed his voice to stay on the cross, as he winnowed my path, I learned so much more about relationships, reputation and image. My heart now is flooded with gratitude as I look at my congregation, a wonderful body of people, many of whom stayed, trusted when they couldn't see, and gave encouragement when they needed it themselves – Good Friday people, not Palm Sunday people. What a group of people to build with!

CHAPTER 13

The Giant of Ministerial Jealousy

David did not waste his time fighting the giants of family familiarity or people's opinions, and certainly not that of ministerial jealousy. *1 Samuel 17:32-39* records those words that were screeching in his soul: 'Something needs to be done about this.' He walked into King Saul's tent after being summoned: his words and actions had caused quite a stir in the ranks and been brought to the attention of King Saul, who was now curious to find out who was causing all the commotion. May God raise up more Davids in our churches whose words and actions challenge the apathy, cowardice and selfishness in our ranks.

David stood before the king with a raw, naive passion as he offered his services to go and fight the giant. Saul patronizingly patted David on the head and advised him to put all thoughts of fighting aside: 'You are not able, son, you're just a teenage shepherd, and Goliath is a trained man of war.' David stood his ground, recounting the incident of victory over the lion and the bear. Goliath would share their fate if he could only get his hands on him.

Why did Saul offer his armour to David? I really don't believe it was a gesture of confidence in David. Perhaps it was even to emphasise how ridiculous the idea seemed. Saul clothed David with his armour to humiliate him, to make him and his idea look crazy. Just picture David, trying to walk in this cumbersome metal suit. Saul would shout, 'Over here, David, take a swing at me.' David would take five minutes to change his posture and would be able to turn his head while the heavy helmet remained stationary. Was Saul trying to dampen this young man's spirit by making him look ridiculous and attempting to drain his passion and fearlessness because at that moment such qualities were making Saul look ridiculous? Knowing the flaws in Saul's character exposed in his later life, was there a twinge of jealousy beginning to stir in the king's heart? Were the seeds of envy planted in his heart here, as this young man's courage exposed his cowardice? Perhaps Saul wanted David to wear his armour, thinking, 'Well, he may just pull it off, but if he does it's unthinkable he should get all the credit. If by some amazing good fortune he wins, at least I'll get some credit; he'll be wearing my armour.'

There are a lot of lessons we can learn from this incident, but for me the picture is simple. The older threatened by the younger; the passive jealous of the passionate, and David, whether he was to live or die, prepared to pay the price for his dream. Saul was threatened by David's courage and vision, and the same is happening in the church today. Insecure, threatened leaders, embarrassed and intimidated by passionate, reckless, younger warriors: their naivety frustrates them, their passion embarrasses them, their willingness to die for the cause shames them. So in their attempt not to be seen with egg on their face, they use their experience to humiliate them and their armour to stifle them. Whatever they do, it exposes the main motive – jealousy. This most effective saboteur of success is something we have to recognise and deal with.

Jealousy destroys ministries. Because Saul allowed the seed of jealousy to grow in him, it developed and came into full bloom when the women sang a song praising David's emergence as a warrior: 'Saul has slain his thousands but David his ten thousands.' From that day on, Saul, driven by a tormenting spirit, had only one goal in life: to remove what he thought was the reason for his agony – David.

Jealousy also destroys your relationship with God. When the elder brother of the prodigal son heard the rejoicing at home, welcoming the return of a backslidden brother, it was more than he could bear. Jealousy spread through his whole being and like an octopus' tentacles strangled any love, joy or gratitude that remained. The Bible records in *Luke 15* that rather than join the festivities with his father, *'he refused to go in'*. Perhaps the greatest picture in Scripture of the cancerous power of jealousy is painted in the story of Joseph and his brothers. Jealousy raged like a wild bull in the hearts of Joseph's brothers, until finally they planned to get rid of him. I want to look at the story in this chapter, not to warn you of the dangers of allowing jealousy to rule your heart, but to warn readers who, like David and Joseph, have a dream, a passion and a purpose in life that attracts the green-eyed monster. The question I want to ask is not 'What do I do when I'm jealous?' but 'What do I do when I'm the object of jealousy?'

If we give in to the domination, intimidation and restriction that jealous people put on us, we will fail to take out our Goliath and realise our dreams. David and Joseph are classic examples of what to do when you become the object of jealousy. David did not waste his time fighting the giant of ministerial jealousy, and neither did Joseph. During those fourteen long years of waiting to see his dream realised,

Joseph did not give in to sourness when sold into slavery by his brothers. He did not give in to sensuousness when tempted by Potiphar's wife. He refused to submit to selfishness when he had to work on someone else's dream and, as difficult as it was, self-pity was sent packing when he was overlooked and forgotten. Spitefulness rose up and demanded attention as Joseph stood before his grovelling brothers, but he refused to give it audience. And what of success, as they placed the sceptre of authority in his hand and he rose to the heady height of second-in-command in the most powerful nation on earth? No! To none of these did Joseph bow. He saw his dream realised because he refused to surrender to the pressure of being the object of jealousy. Joseph's greatest victory was not over the darkness of the pit, the treachery of Potiphar's wife, the darkness of prison or the selfishness of the butler and baker. The glamour of success and position was not that much of a problem: I believe his biggest victory was over his brothers' jealousy. Whatever else he had to experience was just the fruit produced by the seeds of jealousy in his brothers' hearts.

You may be reading this and relating to every word, for you find yourself in the same position. All you want to do is serve God, serve people and fulfil your destiny, but from the most unlikely source, jealousy has raised its ugly head and you are its target. You may be a child in school, bullied because of your looks or intellect. You may be an employee at work, shunned because of your excellent spirit, honourable attitude and honest work ethics, qualities that shine a spotlight on the differences in your colleagues. You may even be a church worker or leader who has been favoured by God and placed in a position you neither sought nor asked for, but because of it you are now the object of criticism, gossip and rejection. You are tempted to do something to appease their envy; you want to assure them you're not doing this on purpose, but the more you try to fight this giant, the more it confirms to them they are justified in their actions. Let me help you to stop wasting any more time fighting this giant of jealousy as it is directed towards you, and keep you focused on what you're called to do.

There are two things you will be tempted to do when you are the object of jealousy. **Firstly, you will be tempted to lower your standard of excellence and demean yourself.** One member of my congregation shared a situation that involved their grandson. He moved from primary school into comprehensive school (in my day we used to say we had moved from the small school to the big school). In the small school, their grandson had loved to study, loved homework, loved the teachers. He presented himself well, school was great, and he couldn't wait to get there. After he had attended comprehensive school for a while, his grandparents noticed a difference in his attitude towards what he had once relished. His love of study went, his love of homework went, his respect for his own appearance went. They put it down to teenage adolescent metamorphosis: the weird season kids go through on their journey into adulthood. The real reason surfaced during a conversation with the lad, when he opened up to his grandparents. He told them the kids in his class at the start of the first year were calling him 'Swot' and 'Teacher's pet'. To be accepted by his jealous peers, he gave in to the temptation, lowered his standards and demeaned himself. The grandfather spoke to the teacher. The teacher understood and commented on the noticeable deterioration of his work and appearance. Knowing the boy was full of potential, bright and eager to learn but pressured by a group of jealous children, he decided to place him in another class of children who wanted to excel. The teacher said, 'When he is in the company of other swots, he will want to excel because of the competition.' The lesson is simple: refuse to lower your standards to be accepted by jealous people; find people who have the same aspiration to excellence and the same passion to excel at what they do.

The second thing you will be tempted to do when you are the object of jealousy is to throw away your principles of integrity. A young lady who has lost her virginity will sometimes influence her friend to do so. Why? Because she is jealous of the integrity that has guarded others from making the same mistake. People will pressure you to sacrifice your integrity because they have already lost theirs. They are jealous of the fact that you still have yours. How many people have been sidetracked and sold their dream, simply because they don't want to be an object of jealousy?

How should we react when we become the object of the green-eyed monster? What should our response be? Is there an example to follow? Joseph stands up again and says, 'Hey, do what I did.' You may lose friends, your actions and attitudes may provoke even more criticism, but you will keep moving in the right direction. Joseph had already kindled his brothers' jealousy by telling them about his dream in which they fell at his feet, paying him homage. He said, *'There we were, binding sheaves in the field. Then behold, my sheaf arose and also stood upright; and indeed your sheaves stood all around and bowed down to my sheaf'* (Gen. 37:7). The reaction of Joseph's brothers should have indicated to Joseph, 'If you want to stay alive, stop now.' He was already hated because of the favour his father showed to him, and the brothers 'hated him now even more because of his dreams and for his words.' It was going from bad to worse for Joseph. He was hated for the favour he received, he was hated for the revelation he received and he was hated for the words he spoke. Jealousy was at boiling point.

Stop now, Joseph, try to win your brothers' acceptance, tell them you ate too much cheese, begin to act like a brat to your father, show them you want to be like them. But Joseph did nothing of the sort; he came right back to them and said, *'Look, I dreamed another dream and this time the sun and the moon and the eleven stars bowed down to me.'* Joseph, however unwise we may think he was, was just being himself. He was naively sharing with his brothers what he believed he was destined to be. He didn't know all the details then, he was just 'dreaming out loud.' Bono, lead singer with U2, coined that phrase at their Millennium concert: he said it's time to 'dream out loud.' I'm not talking about arrogantly blowing your own trumpet, but about living and speaking in such a way that people know you have been born for a purpose and that anything that distracts you from fulfilling that purpose has to go. Serving Jesus comes first in your life; seeking his kingdom comes first in your life; finding and fulfilling your destiny comes first in your life. For these reasons you discipline your conduct, you declare your intentions. If people don't like it, if people are challenged by it, if people are jealous of you, then so be it, but don't back off from desiring to excel. Do what Joseph did. Pile on the pressure. **Don't lower your standard to be accepted, raise your standard to be different.** If people are jealous of your success, keep on seeking the favour of God. If people are jealous of your talent, train to excel in that gift. If people are jealous of your integrity, pile on the pressure. If people are jealous of your loyalty, pile on the pressure. If people are jealous of your passion for God, answer them as David answered his wife. She watched as he, from her perspective, made a spectacle of himself while worshipping in public. His reply was, 'I'm going to get even more undignified than this and will be humble in my own sight.' When he was the object of jealousy and ridicule, David, like Joseph, said, 'I will not lower my standards to make you happy. I will not compromise my convictions just because they challenge you. I am going to get worse.' Come on, stop feeling sorry for yourself because you're the object of someone's jealousy. Dream out loud and keep moving.

CHAPTER 14

The Giant of Traditional Methodology

Another of the giants that David refused to fight was the giant of what I call 'Traditional Methodology' or 'You can't do it like that, we have always done it this way.' Saul's armour didn't work for David. Whatever Saul's motive was, his way of doing things was not going to work for David. David humbly tried, he listened, he was not rebellious but he realised that if he was going take Goliath out, he would have to fight him with weapons that had been tried and tested. However unorthodox, however revolutionary, however strange, they were weapons designed for his use. He resisted the pressure to conform to traditional methodology and instead used the gifts, talents and experience that were uniquely his.

Every one of us has been given unique gifts and every one of us has been uniquely prepared to do what God has called us to do. Don't despise your uniqueness. Don't look at your sling and compare it with the sophisticated armour of Saul. It's your sling, you've succeeded with it in the past, you have proved God with it in the past. Don't be intimidated because what God is asking you to use seems small; don't be intimidated because what you hold in your hand seems ridiculous. It's yours, it's been designed for you, it's unique: use it.

God spoke to me clearly during a study time when I was preparing to teach my congregation. I was about to teach from the story in *2 Kings 4* about the widow who had lost her husband. Having been widowed, she had no income coming in, had a son to raise and a house to keep, and was feeling she had come to the end. The creditors were coming to collect on her debt, and if she couldn't meet their demand they were going to take away her son. What a predicament! While she felt she was facing a demand she could not meet, God was about to show her that it was an opportunity brilliantly disguised as an unsolvable problem.

When the man of God met her, she explained she was going to eat her last meal with the little she had left and then die. Elisha asked her a simple question: *'What do you have in your house?'* Her answer exploded in my spirit and from her reply I taught my church for six weeks on one word: **'except'.** *'Your servant has nothing at all. Except a little oil.'* That is all Elisha needed to hear. Look, you have got something, you have an **'except'.** It may not look like anything to you, but when given to God it can become **exceptional.** The Holy Spirit shouted in my heart, 'Ray, tell your people I accept their "excepts". What you see as nothing, I see as material.' What we see as little, God sees as potential. What we see as 'except', God sees as exceptional. Don't despise your excepts. Before you make the decision to give up, look in your house: you will come back to God and say, 'I have nothing *except...*' We all have an except lying around in our home: pick it up and give it to God, because he will accept that except, and use it as the means to deliver you and others.

The Bible is full of incidents where God took what looked small and insignificant, what people viewed as an except. They gave it to God and experienced incredible things. The disciples, facing the impossible task of feeding a crowd of thousands, weighed up the situation, evaluated their resources to meet the need and concluded it was a non-starter. They explained to Jesus that it was too late, the crowd was too large and their means were too small. Jesus said to them, 'Well, what do you have?' 'We have nothing *except* these five loaves and two fishes.' Jesus accepted their except, blessed it, broke it and gave it back to them, and in their own hands they saw what they viewed as *'except'* transform into something exceptional. Jesus asks us the same thing. Just give me something I can break. What are the five loaves and two fishes in your life that you see as nothing, but God sees as potential?

The secret is in the breaking. It was only when the alabaster box containing precious ointment was broken that the aroma filled the house. It is only when a seed is planted in the ground and dies that it produces much fruit. It is only when your excepts are given to Jesus and broken that they can be a blessing to many.

What about Moses? Every morning for forty years, waking up with the memory of how it could have been, living in a wilderness outside and inside, and everyday he looked at those sheep and held his shepherd's staff – a reminder of what a failure he was. This is all I can be trusted with! Yet in one day his destiny changed. During one of those ordinary, routine days in the life of a failure, God broke in. The call of God was a distant memory; the passion for his destiny was a forgotten dream, the plight of his people an irrelevant problem. After forty years meditating on how he had failed, his self-confidence had gone, his belief in his destiny had gone and his fiery zeal had gone. Standing before that bush was a burnt-out man. He had no more fuel to offer God, no more strength, no more dreams or plans. As far as Moses was concerned, he had never felt more unusable. Yet as far as God was concerned, Moses was ready to begin the final and most productive season of his life. He gazed with wonder as the divine fire of God burned in this ordinary bush. What was even more incredible was that the fire did not need its branches as material to perpetuate the flames. Right there, God was making a statement to Moses. 'I'm going to use you, Moses. Just as my presence is burning in this bush, not needing its branches to perpetuate my glory, so I can burn in you, not needing anything you can offer to keep it ablaze. Just as I am speaking through this ordinary bush, a bush you have passed many times before, a bush you have never noticed but which now because of my presence demands your attention, so I will burn in you. I will put the fire of my call in you, a forgotten, burnt-out, overlooked failure, and use you to demand the attention of the enemy and destroy him, freeing my people. Moses, when you were in Egypt I couldn't use you because you were fuelled by your own agenda, your own emotions, ego and strategy, but now after forty years you have no human fuel to offer me. So now my fire can burn as it was meant to, needing no human element to sustain it.'

God may be using this ordinary book with his fire in it to grab your attention and declare to you that it's not over, it's just beginning. Like Moses you stand before the bush with nothing to give *except* a history of failure, a heart that's cold and a hand that holds only an insignificant piece of wood. Keep reading: your life is about to change.

One of the most important keys to cooperating with God as he prepares us and releases us into our assignments is to understand the difference between a burden and a call. Moses had acted passionately forty years earlier to free his people, but he was fuelled by a burden, not a call. The Bible says, *'It came into his heart.'* Acts 7:24-25 says, *'And seeing one of them suffer wrong, he defended and avenged him who was oppressed, and struck down the Egyptian. For he supposed that his brethren would have understood that God would deliver them by his hand, but they did not understand.'* There was nothing wrong with Moses' motive, nothing wrong with Moses' understanding of his mission; what he got wrong was the timing. You will not fulfil your destiny with burden, only with call.

Timing is the incubator that completes the process. You must understand the difference between a burden and a call: it will help you make sense of why you may have failed in the past. It wasn't that God was not with you; it wasn't the fact that you got it wrong concerning the essence of your assignment. It was probably the timing. The burden had not yet developed into a call, a release date or a commission. There are three things that will help you distinguish between a burden and a call:

Firstly, a burden comes and goes but a call stays

When I was a young Christian, I read many books on the lives of missionaries and people who embarked on great exploits for God. One of those was Brother Andrew, who wrote *God's Smuggler.* I was fascinated as I read of the courage he displayed, placing his life in danger to get Bibles to the underground church in China. I was challenged, excited and stirred. I pictured myself doing the same thing. What a great way to spend your life, being the 007 of the church: undercover operations, miraculous intervention by the Holy Spirit, angelic visitation and deliverance. A burden was growing in my heart: 'Let's go do it.' Then I began to read of the things that didn't work out as expected. I began to read of the persecution, loneliness and misunderstanding, and guess what – the burden left. A burden will run when faced with opposition, but a call stays. A burden will run when faced with disappointment. A burden will run when faced with rejection, offence, persecution or failure, but a call stays. To test whether you have a burden or a call, give it some opposition. Give it a

Pharaoh to oppose it, a Red Sea to stop it, a prison to contain it, a wilderness to forget it, some pain to abort it or some suffering to despise it. Give it a cross to kill it. A burden needs fuel to keep it alive: the fuel of appreciation, favourable circumstances and applause. A call only needs God. Notice the difference in Moses, impassioned by a burden, then fuelled with a call. After the encounter with God at the burning bush he still had to face an uncooperative people and a stubborn enemy, on top of which he was fighting his own internal war of inferiority and inadequacy. Yet this time he didn't run. Why? This time the burden of his heart became a call from God's heart.

Secondly, a burden has options but a call has no choice

When trouble arrives, burden-driven people start looking for options. Check out the Israelites at the Red Sea. Even after their miraculous deliverance, they were complaining to Moses as they seemingly came to a dead end. The first problem they had had to face since their deliverance, the Red Sea before them and Pharaoh on their heels behind them, yet all memory of God's amazing miracles in Egypt forgotten, all memory of the atrocious conditions they had lived in forgotten. All they could say was, *'It would have been better for us to serve the Egyptians' (Ex. 14:12)*. That's how you differentiate between burden-driven people and call-driven people. Burden-driven people start looking for options. They want miracles without the muck, deliverance without disturbance, favour without rejection and prosperity without sacrifice. Call-driven people have no option; they are faced with the same temptation to selfishness, but they have nowhere to go but forward, no one to rely on but God. What if Jesus had said on the cross, 'It would have been better for me if I had stayed in heaven'? What if Paul had said in the Philippian jail, 'It would have been better for me to have stayed a Pharisee'? What if John had said on the isle of Patmos, 'It would have been better for me if I'd kept my mouth shut'? What if Daniel had said in the lions' den, 'It would have been better for me if I'd worshipped that idol'? Let me ask you this question: 'Is your burden being tested?' If you've been saying, 'It would have been better for me,' I would question whether you have been called. The call of God is not about me: *'Not my will but your will be done.'* Call-driven people have no options. They have burnt their bridges and their boats. There is nowhere to go but forward.

Thirdly, the call of God is the reason for your gifting

God hasn't given you gifts and talents and a process of preparation just so that you can feel good or look good. It's to enable you to fulfil your call. Let me show you something powerful. John the Baptist declared that Jesus would give us a double-barrelled baptism: *'I baptize you with water,'* he declared, *'but one mightier than I is coming, whose sandal strap I am not worthy to loose. He will baptize you with the Holy Spirit and fire' (Mt. 3:11).* There is a very important revelation here that will help you in relation to gifting and calling. Jesus baptizes us with the Holy Spirit and fire. One is related to gifting, the other to calling. When one hundred and twenty people were filled with the Holy Spirit in an upper room in Jerusalem, the Bible says not only did they speak in other tongues, gifted by God, but over each of them sat a tongue of fire – called by God. Jesus declared to a shocked group of Jews in his home town of Nazareth, *'The Spirit of the Lord is upon me.'* **Gifting** *because* **calling**. The devil is not so concerned about you operating in your giftings, but he really gets terrified when you begin to channel them into your call – the fire. Petrol spilled on the ground and set alight can create quite an attraction, but petrol channelled into a car will actually achieve something, take you somewhere, help someone. There are many Christians running around operating gifts, conducting meetings, busy with activity, but they don't really achieve anything because they need the fire of calling to channel them.

It was the fire that made the bush like no other bush. As long as the fire burned in that bush, three things were evident:

The fire gave the bush authenticity – it grabbed Moses' attention.

The fire gave the bush distinctiveness – it was not like all the other ordinary bushes.

The fire gave the bush vitality – the fire burned in the centre but its branches were not consumed.

If you have lost your sense of authenticity, distinctiveness, identity, vitality, joy and strength it is very possible that you have moved away from the fire. You have neglected to allow the fire to burn in you and it is time to fan into flame your gifting and calling. In 1986, after six years of preaching, travelling and singing in schools, on street corners and in churches, I was feeling a little tired and spiritually jaded. My gift was operating but there was something missing. I felt I was functioning on automatic pilot. One night I sat in a church and listened to someone advertise a conference in Harare, Zimbabwe. When I heard the theme of the conference, my ears went up like Dumbo the elephant's. 'The Fire Conference' – that's it, I thought, that's what I need. Miraculously God provided for me to go, and for a week in the early part of 1986 I sat at the feet of Reinhard Bonnke and others, to receive everything I could. I felt as if I was sitting there with a funnel on my head, receiving everything I felt I could contain. My life was changed. I received a fire that needed no fuel. From that time I realised I no longer had to fuel my calling with my own emotions, willpower or personality; God had given me a fire that burned with or without human help.

My first appointment after that encounter was to sing at the Assemblies of God Annual Conference in Minehead. I was to sing in the middle of a business meeting, to break things up. That's exactly what happened! The Lord showed me prior to entering the meeting what was about to take place. In a vision I saw people falling down in repentance, being thrown back with the power of God, pastors crying out for a baptism in fire. I was so excited, but the Holy Spirit told me that for this to take place I would have to say certain words. I agreed and walked into the meeting with incredible expectancy. I asked the leader of the meeting if I would be allowed to say a few words before I sang. He reluctantly agreed and I waited for my turn to sing. The meeting progressed according to the planned programme, nothing special, in fact very routine. My spirit was burning with anticipation with what God was about to do. I was introduced as the 'singing item' and as I took the microphone in my hands, I repeated exactly what God had told me to say. 'Servants of God,' I started, 'God has told me to tell you he loves you. He also told me to tell you this. He has not baptized you in denominationalism, he has not baptized you in theology, he has baptized you with the Holy Ghost and fire. **You have been fanning the wrong flame**. After I sing this song called "Take off the mask", many of you will open up to the Holy Ghost as he comes to fill this place with his fire.' I sang the song and the fire came. I saw what I had seen in the vision God gave me. The business meeting was turned into a revival meeting. The programme was abandoned as people cried out to God and received fresh fire. It was wonderful.

There is a strategic plan of the devil to target men and women of fire and lure them away from their position of calling. God showed me this by revelation while I was reading *1 Samuel 13:19-20: 'Now there was no blacksmith to be found throughout all the land of Israel, for the Philistines said, "Lest the Hebrews make swords or spears." But all the Israelites would go down to the Philistines to sharpen each man's ploughshare, his mattock, his axe and his sickle.'* **Satan's strategy is still the same, 'removing the blacksmiths'.** The Philistines realised that instead of using their energy in planning and suffering potential losses as a result of an all-out battle with the armies of Israel, they could just remove the people who were responsible for equipping and sharpening their weapons – the blacksmiths. It proved very effective, because on the day of the battle 'there was neither sword nor spear found in the hand of any of the people'. Satan's strategy is still the same. To whom has God allotted the task of *'equipping of the saints for the works of ministry' (Eph. 4:12)*? To apostles, prophets, evangelists, pastors and teachers, ministry gifts – blacksmiths, men and women of fire. If a blacksmith is to do his job successfully he has to stay by the fire. For the enemy to do his job successfully, all he has to do is lure them away from their place of effectiveness, the fire, their calling. Those of you reading these words who are ministry gifts called to be people of fire, honing, sharpening and equipping God's army: has Satan lured you away from your place of effectiveness? We need every blacksmith to be in place. If you have moved, get back to where you belong – the fire.

It is interesting that the Philistines didn't stop the blacksmiths sharpening their social implements. It was their battle instruments they were instructed not to sharpen. Why is it we have moved away from spiritual gifts to social skills? We are more concerned with developing our counselling technique than our spiritual arsenal. A word of knowledge will save you and those you are helping a lot of time. A prophetic word from God will do far more than three weeks learning how to understand the various personality types. Where are the blacksmiths? Where are the men and women of fire? Get back to the bush. Get back to your place of calling.

God broke into a normal day in Moses' life in *Exodus 3:1*. It says, *'Now Moses was tending the flock of Jethro.'* Moses was *'tending'*, just as he had done for forty years, just an ordinary day. He got up that morning with no unusual sense of expectancy, no word from God in his daily reading, nothing unusual, just another ordinary day in the life of a forgotten failure.

It is interesting that if you were to run a check on many of the people God has chosen and used mightily, you would find the same thing happened to them. God just broke into one of their normal days and revolutionised their lives. Paul was riding his horse, David was working for his father, the disciples were mending their nets, Mary could have been washing her hair. One of the most amazing stories that illustrate what I'm trying to communicate to you concerns the German evangelist Reinhard Bonnke. After finishing his studies at the Bible College of Wales in Swansea he was on his way back to his parents' home in Germany. He had a few hours to spare in London while waiting for his ferry, so he decided to do some sightseeing. I will let Reinhard tell it in his own words, as recorded in the book *Reinhard Bonnke, a Passion for the Gospel.*

The train from Swansea took Reinhard Bonnke to London where he had a few hours to spare before the next stage of his journey to the overnight ferry. He was told the time-honoured way of seeing London was by the world-famous red London buses. Having enough money for a run-about ticket, he travelled the streets of the capital, changing buses at random. He was free, he was going home, and life and London looked wonderful from the top deck of a double-decker bus.

After an hour or two he needed exercise, so he alighted at the next stop and strolled down the road, with little idea where he was except that he was still within the bus routes of London. As he enjoyed the walk, a sign informed him that this area was called Clapham. The name meant nothing to him and he walked on until he found himself outside a house with a wooden fence around it and on it a board bearing the name, Principal George Jeffreys. He stopped in his tracks and looked at the name again. It was there clear enough, but no; he dismissed it, it could not be. Only a few weeks earlier, he had been browsing through the books in the college library when he chanced upon Healing Rays by George Jeffreys. His interest was quickly aroused as he scanned through the contents.

It was a balanced scriptural exposition on the subject of divine healing. The final chapter was full of testimonies of miracles in the ministry of George Jeffreys, which were witnessed by huge congregations in the largest halls throughout the British Isles. The founder and leader of the Elim Foursquare Gospel Alliance, he had clearly been a greatly anointed evangelist.

Reinhard had been absorbed, but he noted that the miracles mostly occurred in the 1920s. He presumed that this great evangelist must be dead, and when he had left college, George Jeffreys had been far from his thoughts. But now he wondered. Was it possible that this great evangelist was still alive and lived here? He had almost decided that it was nonsense even to think so, when the Holy Spirit seemed to whisper in his heart, 'Why don't you find out?'

Contrary to what people may think when they see him in action on a platform, Reinhard is not one to rush into things; he likes to think before he acts. But at once he knew he must know the truth. He went up to the front door and rang the bell. Just when he was beginning to think that there was no one in, a woman opened the door.

'Excuse me,' he asked, 'but I saw the nameplate and wondered, is this the home of George Jeffreys, the mighty evangelist who reached a whole nation?'

'Yes, it is the same man,' she replied.

'Please, do you think that I may see him? I have just finished at Bible College and I am on my way home to Germany.'

Her reply was an unpromising 'No', and with that she started to close the door, when a voice echoed from within, 'Let him come in.'

In went the wondering Reinhard and there, coming down the stairs, was the frail figure of an elderly man. In a deep husky voice, he greeted Reinhard and asked him what he wanted. Reinhard explained how he had just finished Bible College and the call of God was on his life to be a missionary in Africa. He was led into one of the rooms, and invited to sit down. George Jeffreys sat down opposite him on a couch and began to ask Reinhard lots of questions about himself. The fact that Reinhard had been at college in Wales helped to open the conversation with this Welsh preacher whose roots were in the Great Revival there in 1904, and the conversation ignited with the fire of a spiritual rapport which obliterated the generation gap. It was a meeting of two kindred souls with a mutual passion for evangelism. One who was reckoned by many to be the greatest British evangelist of this century, who knew he was coming to the end of his life. The other an eager young man who knew that God had given him the ministry of an evangelist, taking up the mantle of his ministry.

Suddenly the old man slid onto his knees, pulling Reinhard down with him. The glory of God came on Reinhard as George Jeffreys laid his hands upon his head and prayed for him. The tired but still eloquent voice gained in strength as the old Welsh revivalist poured out his soul in prayer for the raw and eager young man whom God had brought to his house for him to bless. He, who had spent his life beseeching sinners to receive Christ, was again seeking the face of God for the lost, but through the ministry of this young German kneeling with him.

149

Did God give George Jeffreys a glimpse into the future ministry of Reinhard Bonnke? Was he allowed a foresight of the tremendous expansion of the revival which was just at hand? We cannot know, but when Reinhard finally rose from his knees he knew that he had received something powerful from God. He left the house dazed at what had happened as the housekeeper closed the door behind him.

He could not take it all in. He had not even had George Jeffreys on his mind, yet in a city of around ten million people God had brought him to the man's door. The more he thought about it the more he thanked God for so leading him.

What an amazing encounter! You see, the wonderful thing about God is that he never forgets why we were born. God never forgot why Moses was born. He was born at the worst possible time, right in the middle of the rule of an Egyptian tyrant who was slaughtering every baby he could find. Moses was supernaturally protected in the Nile, was raised in Pharaoh's house, received the cream of Egypt's knowledge. Educated at the Oxford of the then greatest world power, he studied mathematics, astronomy, geometry and music. He was a trained fighting machine and a skilled orator, and he developed many other qualities during the first forty years of his life. The forty years in Egypt and the forty years in the wilderness, although in complete contrast, were both necessary in God's plan for Moses' preparation. God would never have invested all that in Moses for nothing.

God never forgot why Moses was born. Although your life may be full of contrasts, every colour is needed to complete the painting; every scene is needed to finish the synopsis. The tapestry of our lives from our perspective may look like a jungle, an uncoordinated thread, but from God's perspective it is perfect.

Very often the principles of destiny are only really understood with hindsight. Very often the most difficult time is when you are actually in the process of discovery. When you think you're going backwards, you're actually going forwards. When you think you're being crushed, you're actually being built up. When you're seemingly failing, you're actually succeeding. When you think you've missed it, you have actually hit the bull's-eye. It's only when you consider the whole of your life up to this point that you realise God has taken every thread, the good, bad, ugly, joyful and painful, and woven it into the tapestry of your life's calling. Wonderful!

God called from within the bush, 'Moses, Moses': God never forgot his name. Eighty years earlier, a young Egyptian maid had lifted him tenderly out of the Nile and called him Moses, which means 'Drawn out'. During those forty years in the wilderness, Moses could have renamed himself 'Failure', 'Inadequate', 'Unusable', but God reminded him of his name and with it the realisation that he was born for a purpose. He had been drawn out of a hostile environment, against all odds kept alive and prepared for this moment. Even though you have been through many trials, endured many hostile environments, suffered many disappointments and failure, God has not forgotten your name. It is written in a book in heaven with the indelible blood of Jesus. Persecution cannot erase it, nor pain, failure, self-doubt or the passing of time. It is time to answer and respond as he calls your name and asks you to give him what it is you have in your hand.

This is where we really begin to panic. When we realise God has not forgotten us, that he has a plan for us, a destiny, an assignment, we also realise we have nothing *except* a stick. After Moses had realised this was not a dream, that what he had thought was dead was now being resurrected, he nevertheless felt totally unprepared and absolutely unequipped. His excuses poured out of his mouth: 'I messed up before, I can't speak. What if they won't listen to me, what if they think I'm delusional and I'm making all this up? I've got nothing to give you or them.' God listens patiently, then asks Moses, *'What is that in your hand?* Cast it on the ground. Give it to me.' As Moses stood before God, having run out of reasons why he couldn't be used, God was looking at his 'except'. You've told me what you don't have, Moses; what do you have?' 'Well, I have nothing except this stick,' Moses replies, and God says, 'I accept your except: just give it to me and I'll show you what I can do'. As Moses handed over that rod, he was handing over to God something he had used for forty years. It was something that had become so familiar to him that he even forgot he was holding it during that encounter with God. 'I've got nothing,' he was saying, forgetting what he was holding in his hand. 'This rod? How can you want this rod? For forty years it's become part of my person, it's nothing special. I use it to tend the sheep and fight off wolves; it helps me to walk over the rocky terrain. It never leaves my side, it's always with me; it's like an extension of my arm. It's something that comes naturally to me!'

Exactly, it's the things that are familiar to us, gifts we have that just come naturally to us, that we see as our 'except'. Many people are looking for something spectacular and super-spiritual and they ignore what they do best. They see nothing special in the things that just come naturally to them. We are like people trying to get into a thirty waist when we are a forty-two. We try to walk on our hands instead of using what was designed for the purpose. 'Moses, what's in your hand?' 'Oh, it's only something I have used for forty years. I have nothing except this rod.' God says, 'I'll take it. I'll accept your except. Give me what comes naturally to you. With it you will embarrass Egypt, part the Red Sea, bring water from a rock and win battles.'

Don't despise what comes naturally to you. Who do you think arranged it that way? Who do you think gave you those natural abilities? Give them to God. I shared this with one of my secretaries one day. With tears in her eyes she said, 'Pastor, all these years I've wanted to do something special for God, but I have nothing to give him except my office skills; only now have I realised he has taken what comes naturally to me and uses it every day to bless many.' If I tried to type it would take a whole day to write one page, but she could type with her eyelids, without thinking. It wasn't special to her, it was an 'except'. What are you saying to God, as he speaks to you from this burning bush? I've got nothing except a smile? I have nothing except being hospitable, looking after children, playing an instrument, tending a car park? Whatever it is, it is particular to you. It's your sling. It may not look like much to others and you may never have thought God would use it to do something great. Take courage from David: refuse to fight the battle of traditional methodology. Refuse to be intimidated by Saul's armour and give God your except. Samson had nothing except a jawbone, Jesse had nothing except a shepherd boy, Elijah had nothing except a cloud the size of a man's hand, the disciples had nothing except five loaves and two fishes. The Holy Spirit has nothing but a cross, but he continues to change millions of lives because of it.

CHAPTER 15

The Giant of General Consensus

The last of the giants David refused to give in to was the Giant of General Consensus, or the Giant of Crowd Mentality. The majority are not always right. However, when you have a large group of people thinking the same way, acting the same way, speaking the same way, it takes a lot of courage and strong conviction to stand out against such negative unity. How would you have felt, standing in the judgement court in Jerusalem while the Governor sentenced two men before you, one to be freed, the other to be executed? As the chance was offered, with intimidating force, all around united with one voice and began to shout, 'Barabbas, give us Barabbas!' Even though your conviction and belief caused you to shout 'Jesus', the sheer volume of general consensus would drown you out. Doctor Luke records the scene in *Luke 23:18: 'And they all cried out at once, saying "Away with this man, and release to us Barabbas."'* Verse

23 of the same chapter declares, *'And the voices of these men and of the chief priests prevailed.'*

As David stood, surrounded by the Israelite army, there were no shouts of 'Go for it David, we're behind you all the way.' No! The atmosphere was thick with negativity and fear. What David did that day displayed courage and character of the highest level. Not only was he facing the scariest of opponents and the whole Philistine army, but he also stood in the middle of an onslaught from his own side. Not only did he ignore the giants of family familiarity, people's opinions, ministerial jealousy and traditional methodology, but he was also surrounded by a bunch of cowards exuding a spirit of fear that was positively claustrophobic.

1 Samuel 17:23-24 sets the scene: *'Then as he talked with them, there was the champion, the Philistine of Gath, Goliath by name, coming up from the armies of the Philistines; and he spoke according to the same words. So David heard them. And all the men of Israel, when they saw the man, fled from him and were dreadfully afraid.'*

The general consensus, expressed in that attitude and action, shouted at David, 'You're crazy, this will never work: go back home.' David had to overcome both the threatening shouts of the enemy and the negative shouts of those who were supposed to be his support. That's where you may be right now. The general consensus says, 'It can't be done. Who do you think you are? You're doomed to fail, so don't even try' – and those are just the comments from your supporters. On top of that, the enemy who stands between you and your fulfilled dream is there defying, taunting and intimidating you. If so, this chapter will help you to resist the temptation to fight the giant of general consensus. Ignore the pathetic attempts of the enemy to intimidate you and run toward your purpose, shouting, *'You come to me with sword and spear and javelin, but I come to you in the name of the*

Lord of hosts, the God of the armies of Israel whom you have defied.' David stood in the middle of two camps, one group defying God, the other denying him, but David, who is a perfect type of faith in action, overcame both and won the day.

Let me show you an interesting and powerful analogy that gives you a picture of how your faith works. Using this simple story, let me take the liberty of replacing David's name with 'faith' and you will clearly see the mechanics of this spiritual muscle called faith.

There are nine things you should know about your faith. **Firstly, faith is your servant.** Put yourself in Saul's shoes for a moment and you will understand what I mean. Saul was sitting in his tent, and he had a problem – a big problem. In comes a little shepherd boy who says these amazing words: *'Let no man's heart fail because of him; your servant will go and fight this Philistine' (1 Sam. 17:32).* That's exactly what your faith says to you as you face your giants. In the Old Testament, kings and priests had servants to do their work. The same applies in the New Testament. We have been made kings and priests and we too have a servant who wants to work for us.

Faith works! *1 John 5:4* declares, *'This is the victory that overcomes the world, even your faith.'* Instead of sending out doubt, negativity and fear, send out your faith. It will work for you. It worked for the four men who brought their paralysed friend to be healed: *'And Jesus, seeing their faith, said unto the man, "Son, be of good cheer: your sins are forgiven."'* Faith serves, faith works, faith overcomes; faith can be seen. It worked for the woman with the issue of blood. She pressed through a hostile crowd with an incurable disease and touched his clothes, releasing the supernatural power of God. Jesus, knowing someone had sent out the servant of faith, said, *'Who touched me?'* When she was identified, these immortal words came from his mouth: *'Daughter, your faith has made you well. Go in peace.'* Your faith has made you well! Not the revelation of my love for you, not the size of the crowd, not your proximity to me, but your faith. It's time to let your faith serve you, work for you, overcome for you, touch God for you. Like David, he is shouting in your spirit: 'Don't worry about the situation you're facing. Send me out, let me at it; your servant will go and fight for you.'

Right now, faith is standing up in your spirit, saying, 'Let me deal with your giants, that's what I'm here for.' **That's the second thing faith wants to do for you: he wants to deal with your giants.**

The third thing faith wants to do is to keep fear from dominating your heart. David confidently tells Saul, *'Let no one lose heart.'* Faith always says, *'Fear not.'* When your heart is full of faith, fear can't park. Have you ever been waiting in line behind twenty cars to enter a multi-storey car park? You arrive at the ticket stand and you have to wait another ten minutes because there is a flashing sign saying 'Car park full.' You have to wait for a car to leave before a ticket is issued, allowing you in. The same principle applies to your heart. The best way to keep intruders out of your life is to keep your life full and give them no room. Unforgiveness has to stay outside because you're full of grace. Deception has to stay outside because you're full of truth. Resentment has to stay outside because you're full of love. Depression has to stay outside because you're full of joy, and fear has to stay outside because you're full of faith.

The fourth thing we see is that faith can be hindered from working. As Goliath gazed down on this pathetic attempt to take him out, as he saw this youngster run toward him, I'm sure he admired David's courage but was deeply offended by the challenge. He bellowed across the battlefield, intending to intimidate David, 'You're only a boy, you're not big enough to deal with me. Look how big I am compared to how big you are. Go back and come at me when you're bigger.' Is that what your giant is shouting at you? 'What you're sending out to defeat me is too small. Come back when you're bigger'. Don't listen to him. One of the ways you can hinder your faith working is to confess that it's too small. The wonderful thing about this visual picture of huge Goliath and little David is that it confirms the words Jesus said when the disciples pleaded with him to increase their faith: *'If you have faith as small as a mustard seed,'* he declared, *'you would be able to say to this mountain, be removed and cast into the sea and it would obey you.'* Did you hear that? Mustard seed versus mountain, David versus Goliath, small problem versus big problem. God says to you, 'Don't ask me to increase your faith; use what you have. It's able.' *Reinhard Bonnke* has this wonderful saying: *'How many mustard seeds can you get in your pocket, and how many mountains?'* Compared to your problem, your faith looks as ridiculous as a shepherd boy with a sling, but whatever you do, don't agree with the enemy and say it's too small. You will watch him winning the day for you. Not only was he facing intimidation from the enemy, but also negativity from his own side. 'You're not able,' they declared, to go against the Philistine to fight him. Don't ever listen to those negative cowards, whoever they are. Not only is your faith big enough, he's more than able.

Tell that to God's heroes in Hebrews 11, God's Hall of Fame. Faith enabled Noah to build an ark. Faith enabled Abraham to leave the familiarity of his own country and follow God into the unknown. Faith caused Moses to reject the success of Egypt and identify with his people. Israel crossed the Red Sea because of it. Jericho fell before Joshua because of it. No, don't ever say faith is not able. In your present situation he is the only one who is able. Your personality won't beat the giant, your education won't do it, your friends won't defeat it: faith is the only thing that's able.

Fifthly, your faith can be hindered from working if you weigh him down. We read in *1 Samuel 17:38-39* that Saul attempted to get David to wear his armour. David tried it but was rooted to the spot because of the weight of it. Faith needs nothing to clothe it. We ask faith to fight for us but then we clothe him with our armour. We think he needs a little help, so we put the breastplate of fear on him, not understanding that fear weighs faith down. We put on him the helmet of reason, and give the sword of manipulation and the buckle of worry, not realising that all this stuff that comes from our head and our heart clutters our faith and restricts his movement. Faith uses his own weapons. We read that all David needed was a staff, a stone, a pouch and a sling. Faith needs a staff. Faith comes from and needs the staff of the Word to lean on, as it does not come from the hearing of testimonies. They may encourage faith but they don't produce it. Faith comes by hearing and by learning the Word of God. Faith needs a stone. There are two wonderful pictures here as David reaches down into the stream and picks out five smooth stones. Five in Scripture generally indicates grace. Faith needs grace to work. The Bible says we are saved by grace through faith. *Galatians 5:6* declares, *'For in Christ Jesus neither circumcision nor uncircumcision avails anything, but faith working through love.'* I also noticed that the stones didn't just jump into David's hand: he reached down into the stream and searched for what he needed. The five smooth stones didn't just lie there. They lay amongst lots of other types of stones, but David knew what he needed in order to take Goliath out, he knew the type and size of stone that would fit his sling and reach its mark. The special word that you need to deal with your problem is not just going to jump at you from the Bible: you have to prayerfully read the Word, asking the Holy Spirit to show you the right stone to pick – the scripture you need for the particular problem you're facing. On many occasions when I have been facing massive giants seeking to destroy me, I have gone to the stream of God's provision – the Word – and searched within its flow for stones to fit my sling, and he has always showed me where they are. There are smooth stones, particular stones, right stones to fit your sling, just waiting for you to discover, pick up and use them. They are lying there for you; not for anyone else, but designed for you, to deal with your problem. Take the time to find them. When David found the stones, he placed them in his pouch. He needed a storage space for those stones while he engaged in battle. Faith needs a storage space for the living word of grace. Jesus said, 'If you abide in Me and My words abide in you, you can ask what you will and it will be given you.' Look at the exhortation in *Colossians 3:16: 'Let the word of Christ dwell in you richly.'* Likewise *1 John 2:14* declares, *'I have written to you, young men, because you are strong, and the word of God abides in you, and you have overcome the wicked one.'*

Many ask faith to fight for them, but when he reaches into the pouch to find ammunition, it's empty. Faith cannot fight with just a heart full of good intentions or spiritual feelings: it needs stones. Not only do you need to read the Word, you also need to store it. Musing, memorising and meditating on the Word helps keep your pouch full, so when faith needs it, all it has to do is reach inside, find what it needs and use it. Once he finds the stone needed, he places it in his sling, skilfully aims, and delivers the fatal blow.

The living word of grace is no threat to Goliath while still in the pouch: it needs something to propel it, someone to aim it. *Romans 10:9* enlightens us here: *'If you confess with your mouth . . . you will be saved.'* With the sling of confession you are saved. The heart stores it and the mouth throws it. Don't starve your faith; give him what he needs, let him find in your heart the five smooth stones he needs and let him find in your hand a sling to throw it. The Bible says, 'Life and death are in the power of the tongue.' It's time to throw those stones at the enemy with your tongue. David did not aim the stones at the wrong enemy; he was focused and used his sling wisely – and so should we.

In the heat of battle your faith will encourage you. As David was challenged by the unbelieving crowd concerning his credentials and ability, he began to recount past victories: *'Your servant has killed both lion and bear; and this uncircumcised Philistine will be like on of them,' he said (1 Sam. 17:36).* Let faith do the same for you in the heat of battle when his credibility is questioned. Let faith encourage you from past victories. Remember when you were up against it, remember when you thought you wouldn't make it: but you're still here, ready to fight another day. Allow your faith to encourage you from your past triumphs.

I have realised that one thing that can sometimes cause us to back off in the heat of battle, as our faith runs into the fray, is that the problem becomes bigger before it can be eliminated. As David ran towards Goliath (I love it!), every step made Goliath become even bigger. Many of us shout at our problem, attacking our giants, only to discover that the problem becomes much bigger as we attempt to eliminate it. Some people are attacking personal giants of unproductive habits, relationship strife or financial barriers, and as faith takes each step closer, so the giant not only refuses to move but also gets bigger and more abusive. Don't be intimidated at the stage when you send your faith out, and even though the problem gets a lot bigger, don't call your faith back. Don't change your confession; don't let doubt and negativity and the size of the problem overwhelm you. Faith will win the day for you. *1 Samuel 17:49* records for ever that it did for David.

Hebrews 11:1 declares that *'Faith is the substance of things hoped for, the evidence of things not seen.'* David knew the moment he started out that day that he was going to be the last man standing. Saul's hope was a dead giant: his servant David ran out to make it a reality. If Saul had called David back, he would never have known the joy of victory for himself and the nation. David did not come back defeated, with his tail between his legs, but victorious, with Goliath's head between his hands. Don't call your faith back: he knows the victory is secure. While David was busy dealing with Saul's giant, Saul was in his tent, resting. That's exactly what you need to do while your faith, which you have sent out, confronts and defeats your giants: rest. *Hebrews 4:9-10* says, *'There remains therefore a rest for the people of God. For he who has entered His rest has himself also ceased from his works as God did from His.'* Why are you still fretting over the outcome of your present battle? Send your David out; and when you do, don't call him back, let him use his own weapons. You rest in the sure knowledge that 'this is the victory that overcomes the world, even your faith.' Let your faith fight for you and bring into reality what you hope for.

CHAPTER 16

The Importance of Confidence

As we have studied the detailed and particular preparation that God moulded into David's life, we have seen how it enabled him to defeat Goliath. We have also learned the necessity of patience, faithfulness and wisdom, and finally, and very importantly, the necessity of confidence. The one thing above everything else that really impressed me as I read through *1 Samuel 17*, this amazing encounter between a young boy and a brutal giant, was David's confidence. We see from *1 Samuel 17:45-47* that he was obviously incredibly confident in his God, but just as importantly, he was confident in his own unique preparation. Look at what *1 Samuel 17:40* tells us he did when he collected his stones: he *'put them in a shepherd's bag, in a pouch which he had, and his sling was in his hand.'*

That shepherd's bag represented and symbolised his own unique preparation. Every one of us has our own 'shepherd's bag', our own unique journey preparing us for our particular race. We have all come different ways, from different backgrounds, with different experiences and training to equip us for our own special destiny. As I renew my own journey, on many occasions I have been tempted to put on another's armour because I felt my 'shepherd's bag' wasn't sufficient. What I have come to realise is that if I am to function the way God designed me to, I have to have confidence in my 'shepherd's bag'.

As for my own unique preparation, when I first started my schools ministry I would preach the gospel to young people in such a way as not to offend my Christian friends and peers. I would be very religious and speak to these searching young people in the way I would speak to Christian youth, using phrases that were easily understood by believers but totally alien to my young unsaved audience. Then, with much misunderstanding and criticism from the Christian world, I started to fight from my 'shepherd's bag'. The years spent entertaining in the rock group, my particular sense of humour and my natural ability to communicate were employed to their fullest and the results were amazing. Unorthodox, yes; offensive to some religious people, yes. This was my shepherd's bag and it worked for me. I discovered that I had to maximise the brief time I was given, usually only five to ten minutes, to communicate the gospel in a relevant, palatable way, allowing the power of the gospel to have its full effect. As I sat there, a being from another generation facing a thousand complete strangers, I began to realise the invisible wall of acceptance had to be broken down within the first minute if the hearts of these young people were to be reached. I fully understand that before people accept your message they have to accept you, so I had to find a way to stand before a group of prepared, receptive hearts.

The secret was discovered accidentally while I was being introduced by the headmaster as 'a Christian coming to address the assembly on a religious topic', which only built the invisible wall higher. I felt something inside my nose causing it to itch like crazy, and as I attempted to relieve the itch with a well-targeted scratch with my finger, I heard ripples of laughter peal across the assembly hall. I quickly realised the audience of bored teenagers thought I was doing the unthinkable behind the headmaster's back – picking my nose. I had stumbled upon the divine key to demolish this wall of unacceptance even before I stood to my feet. Nose-picking! The headmaster, still in the middle of introducing his guest speaker, was totally oblivious of the reason for his pupils' inappropriate sniggering in assembly. I continued to be the morning's clown, exaggerating each scratch vigorously, and every time the headmaster turned round to try to discover the source of disturbance he found me looking back at him in total innocence and, like himself, totally bemused as to the reason for the pandemonium. When he returned his attention to the assembly, I proceeded with the new-found key God had given me to open up the hearts and minds of my hearers, taking my acceptance level well up on the 'I like this guy' acceptometer. Jumping off the stage during one of the songs and singing a love song on bended knees to the most hated female member of staff was another key I used to great effect. Some of my communication techniques may be a little different from the norm, but it's my shepherd's bag; it's the way God has prepared me and moulded me to be the type of vessel he desires.

It is amazing: I have preached in many prestigious churches and conferences all over the world and it seems that by the grace of God I can get away with things that would cause most others never to be invited back. It's just a reminder that we're all uniquely prepared and uniquely called. Can I encourage you to take some time out now and think about your 'shepherd's bag': your background, your experiences, your particular personality and journey? God doesn't anoint who you want to be but who you are. Thank God for it and love to be yourself.

As you learn to cooperate with God in this vital area you will develop a confidence which will free you to really be yourself.

David did not only have confidence in his God and his own unique preparation, he also had confidence in his own decisions. David had been under great pressure to make choices that were not his own. They didn't come from his heart, they weren't seeded in his soul as convictions, but as we read *1 Samuel 17:40* we understand David had come to a place where he took control of his own life and decisions. As he was being pressurized to decide according to the conviction of others, it says, *'Then he took **his** staff in **his** hand; and he **chose for himself** five smooth stones from the brook.'* He chose for himself. In his wonderful book *Maximise the Moment* T.D. Jakes writes, *'We cannot underestimate the vital importance of our life's decisions. You must realise that everything you are is the direct result of the decisions you have made or the decisions that were made for you. Like a stone skipped across the smooth glassy surface of a beautiful clear lake, each decision that we make initiates multiple ripples.'* He continues, *'Your life is too precious to leave it in the hands of someone else. We cannot trust our lives to anyone; other people can act as advisors, but never allow someone else's opinion to outweigh our own.'* This is probably one of the hardest principles to learn, especially if you're the type of person who is addicted to being liked or terrified of confrontation. I think there's a little of those traits in all of us, more in some than others; but if we are going to defeat our personal giants, it is imperative that we have confidence in, take the responsibility for, and execute our own decisions.

I think one of the main keys to making good decisions is to understand the source from which they originate. On one occasion, Jesus was giving the disciples a quiz. Having lined them up, he asked them this question: *'Who do men say that I, the Son of Man, am?' (Mt. 16:13).*

Peter, who was the original carrier of 'foot in mouth' disease, on this occasion got it right: *'You are the Christ, the Son of the living God.'* Jesus commended him and said, *'Blessed are you, Simon Bar-Jonah, for flesh and blood has not revealed this to you, but My Father who is in heaven. And I also say to you that you are Peter, and on this rock I will build My church, and the gates of Hades shall not prevail against it' (Mt. 16:17-18).* I can imagine how Peter must have felt in front of the other disciples: really pleased with himself – surely getting that right would make up for many of his botch-ups. But his popularity level didn't last long. Jesus proceeded to prepare their hearts for the future, talking about his predestined path of suffering and execution. Peter couldn't believe what he was hearing. Observing the depressed countenance of his team-mates, and still flying high from his personal commendation from the author of the universe, Peter took it upon himself to disperse this atmosphere of negativity. After all, he was Peter the Rock, the revelation-receiver. 'Enough of this talk, Jesus,' he blurts out, and taking him by the hand he begins patronisingly to explain to Jesus that this is not the way to build team morale. Stopping Peter in mid-flow while he was enjoying the admiring gaze of his confused fellow disciples, Jesus turns to Peter and calmly but firmly calls him by another name. This time it was not Peter the revelation-receiver, the one who got it right, but Satan! *'Get behind me, Satan,'* Jesus said, *'for you are not mindful of the things of God but the things of men. You may have made a good decision during the quiz, but this one is off the wall.'*

I noticed in this particular teaching session of Jesus that within a few minutes he called Peter by three different names. First he was referred to as 'Simon Bar-Jonah', relating to his flesh, his earthly name, then as Peter, the revelation-receiver, his heavenly name, his spiritual side. Thirdly he was referred to as Satan, the demonic influence in his life and decisions. I realised what was happening here, that Peter had the potential of making decisions influenced by three different sources:

Simon – decision seeded and influenced from the flesh.

Peter – decision sourced and directed from the Spirit.

Satan – decision motivated and inspired by the devil.

I then began to understand that the difference between good decisions and bad ones lies in determining the source from which they are made. Simon is Satan's dancing partner. The flesh is not only Satan's inside man, colluding in countless robberies and handing Satan keys to steal precious time and spiritual valuables, but it also hates Peter the revelation-receiver, the Christ in us. In *Galatians 5:16-17* Paul emphasises this by saying, *'Walk in the Spirit, and you shall not fulfil the lust of the flesh. For the flesh lusts against the Spirit, and the Spirit against the flesh;* **and these are contrary to one another,** so that you do not do the things that you wish' (emphasis mine).

The chapter goes on to identify the personality and wants of the flesh, a menu of disgusting potential resident in us all; a potential that needs to be recognised and put to death. We read in *Romans 8: 5-12, 'For those who live according to the flesh set their minds on the things of the flesh, but those who live according to the Spirit, the things of the Spirit. For to be carnally minded is death, but to be spiritually minded is life and peace. Because the carnal mind is enmity against God; for it is not subject to the law of God, nor indeed can be. So then, those who are in the flesh cannot please God. But you are not in the flesh but in the Spirit, if indeed the Spirit of God dwells in you. Now if anyone does not have the Spirit of Christ, he is not His. And if Christ is in you, the body is dead because of sin, but the Spirit is life because of righteousness. But if the Spirit of Him who raised Jesus from the dead dwells in you, He who raised Christ from the dead will also give life to your mortal bodies through His Spirit who dwells in you. Therefore, brethren, we are debtors – not to the flesh, to live according to the flesh.'*

'To be fleshly minded in death,' Paul says: make decisions from the flesh and death is sure. The flesh is not just in a state of disagreement with the Spirit, it is an actual sworn enemy. Paul further clearly explains that if you live your life devoted to the flesh and are influenced to make decisions from this source, **you cannot please God.** The secret to making successful decisions and having confidence in them is to recognise the potential in 'Simon' to take you out of the will of God and encourage 'Peter' to stand up and make decisions to keep you in the will of God.

The struggle for control between Simon (the flesh) and Peter (the Spirit) will continue until we die. So it's time to stop playing 'Simon says' with the devil. Remember the game? 'Simon says put your hands on your head' etc, and the key to winning the game is doing without question what Simon says. In *Luke 22:31-34,* during an amazing conversation with Peter, Jesus shows us just how this battle is a reality: *'And the Lord said, "Simon, Simon! Indeed, Satan has asked for you, that he may sift you as wheat. But I have prayed for you, that your faith should not fail; and when you have returned to Me, strengthen your brethren." But he said to Him, "Lord, I am ready to go with You, both to prison and to death." Then He said, **"I tell you, Peter,** the rooster shall not crow this day before you will deny three times that you know Me"'* (emphasis mine).

Do you notice that in the area of satanic temptation he refers to him as Simon *(Lk. 22:31)*? ***'Simon, Simon!** Indeed, Satan has asked for **you,** that he may sift **you** as wheat.'* Now look just a few verses later (verse 34): 'Then He said, *"I tell **you, Peter,** the rooster shall not crow this day before **you** (Peter) will deny three times that **you** know Me."'* Jesus was in fact saying, 'You will be tempted as Simon but you will deny me as Peter.' In the area of satanic attack and temptation he referred to him as Simon, his earthly name, flesh, but in the area of denial, he referred to him as Peter, his heavenly name, spirit, revelation-receiver, **the one who should know better.** The devil knows that 'greater is he that is in you' than any attack he could throw at you. That's why he never goes for Peter, he goes for Simon – his inside partner, his colleague in crime. The way Satan hinders Peter from making right decisions is by doing an inside job through Simon. The way Satan hinders Peter is through Simon. With this thought in mind, take time out now to read *John 21:1-19* and notice how this particular disciple is referred to as Simon and Peter. Armed with the revelation we have just read, that Satan influences Peter through Simon, I'm going to show you some amazing truth.

CHAPTER 17

Don't Play 'Simon Says' With the Devil

I believe this is a season in the Body of Christ when God desires to circumcise our hearts. It's brutal, uncouth and painful, but it's necessary. God in 'his furious love towards us' desires a relationship with nothing in between. He does not want our spiritual intercourse with him to be desensitised by the flesh around our hearts. The words that follow are not meant to condemn you or leave you feeling useless and hopeless. Whatever issues you're dealing with, whatever besetting sin you're seeking to overcome, whatever incident in your past you're ashamed of, know this: 'Nothing can separate us from the love of God in Christ.' Brennan Manning, in his wonderful book *The Ragamuffin Gospel*, uses this story to illustrate what I mean:

I stand by the bed where a young woman lies, her face post-

operative, her mouth twisted in palsy, clownish. A tiny twig of the facial nerve, the one to the muscles of her mouth, has been severed. She will be thus from now on. The surgeon had followed with religious fervour the curve of her flesh; I promise you that. Nevertheless, to remove the tumour in her cheek, I had to cut the little nerve.

Her young husband is in the room. He stands on the opposite side of the bed and together they seem to dwell in the evening lamplight, isolated from me, private. Who are they, I ask myself, he and this wry mouth I have made, who gaze at and touch each other so generously, greedily? The young woman speaks.

'Will my mouth always be like this?' she asks.

'Yes,' I say, 'it will. It is because the nerve was cut.'

She nods and is silent. But the young man smiles.

'I like it,' he says, 'It is kind of cute.'

All at once I know who he is. I understand and I lower my gaze. One is not bold in an encounter with a god. Unmindful, he bends to kiss her crooked mouth and I am so close I can see how he twists his own lips to accommodate to hers, to show her that their kiss still works.
However ugly you feel inside Jesus twists his lips to let you know I still love you, the kiss still works I'm still passionately for you.

No, the purpose of these closing chapters is to expose 'Simon' for who he is: a thief. He is intent on stealing from you every good thing God has for you. He is a bully, shouting so loud in his desire to drown out the life-giving value of God's Word. He is a mercenary sold out to Satan to obey his command. He is a murderer desiring to kill the life-giving spirit within you. He will jail you in the dungeon of self-pity. He will lead you into the addict's hell. I'm not talking about drug addiction but about praise addiction, where you suffer withdrawal symptoms if you live a short time without flattering words, clapping hands or flashing bulbs.

Darlene Zsech, who is known throughout the world for her incredible anointed worship music, says, *'My biggest enemy is not persecution but admiration.'* Darlene is very well aware of Simon's potential and hunger to feed off the pedestal of prominence, the gaze of admiration and the spotlight of publicity. He is a traitor who will betray Jesus for less than thirty pieces of silver. He will do it for a look or even a thought. He is opposed to, and the enemy of, the Peter in us. He *'lusts against the Spirit', and is an enemy of the Spirit, as a result of which we cannot do the things we wish (Gal. 5:17).*

Paul says, *'In me (that is, in my flesh) nothing good dwells,'* and he declares that there is only one sentence that can be imposed on Simon, and that is death – death on a daily basis. *'For if you live according to the flesh you will die,'* he writes to the Christians at Rome; *'but if by the Spirit you put to death the deeds of the body, you will live' (Rom. 7:13).* As Simon is led away on a daily basis, kicking and screaming, begging for mercy, don't listen to his lying cries, don't give him pardon, for he has the potential to lead you into the prodigal's pigpen, the adulterer's bed, the gossip's web and the liar's lair. He is Satan's dancing partner; he loves the present world. So I exhort you, in the light of this and what you are about to read, don't play 'Simon says' with the devil. As we look at *John 21*, let me show you just how dangerous it is to allow Simon to be the dominating influence in your life.

Firstly, Simon will influence Peter to run away

Look at *John 21:2-3: 'Simon Peter, Thomas called the Twin, Nathanael of Cana in Galilee, the sons of Zebedee, and two others of His disciples were together.* **Simon** *Peter said to them, "I am going fishing." They said to him, "We are going with you also." They went out and immediately got into the boat, and that night they caught nothing.'* Peter had not yet resolved his issue with Jesus.

He was in limbo when it came to his destiny. He was at a standstill. In the middle of this destiny crisis, Simon stood up and led the way. 'I'm going fishing. I'm going back to familiar territory, to where I am in control, where I feel safe, where I can forget, where I can avoid confrontation.' Simon will always influence you to do the same. The flesh hates reality, confrontation and pain.

What is Simon influencing you to run away from? In this case, it was an unresolved relationship problem. What is it with you? Have you gone fishing in the area of a relationship? Is there unresolved tension between you and your spouse, friend or colleague? Hoping it will resolve itself doesn't fix it. Rather than face it, address it and make a decision to confront it: you've 'gone fishing'. Don't let Simon influence you. It's time for Peter to stand up and say enough is enough, this has gone on long enough; it's time to deal with it. Have you gone fishing in the area of an unproductive habit? Something that you have done for so long, you don't even know you're doing it and, worse than that, you allow the Simon in you to excuse it? Rather than face the fact that that unproductive habit has the potential to lead you into sin or cause you to live a compromising lifestyle, Simon convinces you it won't affect you as it does others and he's persuaded you to go fishing. What unproductive habit needs to be addressed and dealt with? Could it be sexual, either in the physical realm or the thought realm? Could it be in the vocal realm – lying, gossiping, negative or critical vocabulary that has become second nature to you? It could be an emotional habit that is causing an unproductive behavioural pattern, wallowing in self-pity, unforgiveness or bitterness. Whatever area it is, don't let Simon influence you to go fishing. Find a trusted friend or minister and allow them to help you to shut Simon up, so that Peter can take his place. Perhaps you have allowed Simon to take you fishing in the sea of unfulfilled vows. You have made a promise to God to commit yourself to something, but either you've never started it or you've only gone halfway through. Instead of paying the price, you've gone fishing.

Don't let Simon take you fishing when you know you have to bring something to a state of closure. Jesus will keep eyeballing you until you deal with it.

Peter sat before a grace-laid breakfast, cooked and prepared by the one he'd denied, every mouthful asking him, 'Why is he doing this? I don't deserve this!' What he didn't realise was that grace was setting him up to bring closure to something: *'He said to him the third time, "Simon, son of Jonah, do you love Me?" Peter was grieved because He said to him the third time, "Do you love Me?" And he said to Him, "Lord, You know all things; You know that I love You." Jesus said to him, "Feed My sheep"'* (Jn. 21:17).

Three times Jesus challenged **Simon** to respond to the ultimate discipleship test: 'Do you love me?' Twice Simon answered, but Jesus, realising there was so much at stake, would not stop the probing question until **Peter** answered. Finally the breakthrough came and closure was reached. For a third time Jesus pressed home the question, *'Do you love me?'* And finally Peter stood up and took responsibility: *'Peter was grieved.'* Finally Peter told Simon to shut up and took responsibility, realising, 'I may have been tempted as Simon but I denied him as Peter'. Until Peter grieves, you cannot move on. I didn't fail as Simon; I failed as Peter, the one who should have known better.

The reason why many can't move on in their destiny is that they have allowed Simon to take them fishing and they avoid facing up to the fact that they failed as Peter, sinned as Peter, gossiped as Peter, denied as Peter, backslid as Peter. The longer you blame Simon, Satan, circumstances or relationships, the longer you will continue to remain at a standstill. Right through this confrontational, probing, heart-searching conversation, Jesus continually reassured Peter his calling was intact, but on hold, until this issue was dealt with. *'Feed my lambs, my sheep;* what I called you to do is still on the agenda,' but it was only after **Peter** grieved and accepted responsibility for his actions that Jesus said 'Follow me'.

What is Jesus eyeballing you over? Don't let Simon answer for you. It's time for Peter to grieve, accept responsibility and hear those hope-filled words: 'Follow me: your destiny is off hold and you're on your way again.'

Secondly, Simon will influence others with his unresolved hurt.

In *John 21:3* we read, 'They said to him, *"We are going with you also."'* How many people have caught others in their whirlpool of self-pity because of unresolved hurt? One of the reasons why you have to deal with Simon in your life is that not only he will suck you under, but he will suck others under also. How many people have left their place in the local church, abandoned their post in a time of need, because they've gone fishing with a Simon, because they've allowed themselves to be sucked in and controlled by the gravitational pull of someone's unresolved hurt? Don't go fishing with a Simon, someone who has left a church with unresolved hurt or issues. Not only did the disciples go with him, but they went 'immediately'. You see, flesh doesn't take time to seek wise counsel. Flesh doesn't check the facts, look below the surface or investigate the truth. Simon is superficial, emotional and shallow.

Thirdly, Simon will lead you into the night to unproductive work.

John 21:3 again: *'And that night they caught nothing.'* The flesh will always lead you into a dark place where nothing is produced. Like Samson, many have been led into the lap of Delilah by Simon and ended up working for the enemy, going around in circles with their eyes gouged out. In her book *Matters of the Heart* Juanita Bynum writes, *'The problem with Samson was not his eyesight but his insight.'* The reason why he lost his strength was not the result of defective eyesight but defective insight. If he had looked inside and reminded himself of who he was and what he was called to do, if his insight had been clear, his eyesight would have been clear. He ended up strapped to a piece of wood, pushing a millstone round and round, a joke to the enemy and an embarrassment to God's people. The good thing about his time of imprisonment was that he had plenty of time to think, remember and regain his insight. As he did, his hair began to grow and grace began to restore, mercy began to work. As he walked round and round, regaining his insight, I can imagine the cry rising up from his heart. But it wasn't for Delilah, it wasn't for pity; it was for another opportunity to prove himself and live as God had intended. God granted his request and the Bible records that he destroyed a whole temple of pagans in one mighty demonstration of supernatural power. He killed more in his death than in all his life.

Sometimes you don't need more opportunity on the outside, you need a season of confinement to regain insight. You may be in a prison as a result of following Simon; you may be in a dark place as a result of following Simon. Take heart; allow the situation to be used by God to restore your insight. Samson regained his insight in a Philistine jail and got back on track. Jonah regained his insight inside a fish's belly and got back on track. The prodigal son regained his insight in a pigpen and got back on track. You may be blinded because of disobedience, rebellion or stubbornness. The greatest thing God can give you is not more sympathy, more opportunity or more power, but more light. What did Joshua ask for to completely destroy his enemy? More soldiers? More power? No! He asked for more light. At his request God stopped the rotation of the earth. He superseded time to give Joshua what he needed – more light. You can kill your enemy with more light.

You can complete your destiny with more light. You can lead yourself and others to victory with more light.

Gordon MacDonald, respected pastor and author of the best-seller *Ordering Your Private World,* was led by Simon out into the night. He fell morally and experienced possibly the darkest season of his life. After his repentance and restoration, he wrote *Rebuilding Your Broken World. He states, 'A respect for the power of evil is a major step toward rebuilding a broken world.'* Jesus said, *'If the light in you is darkness, how great is that darkness?'*

Fourthly, Simon will influence you to live an empty life.

In *John 21:5* we read, *'Then Jesus said to them, "Children, have you any food?" They answered him, "No!"'* The flesh has no appetite for heaven's menu. The Simon in us has no desire for and no understanding of spiritual food. When the disciples returned to find Jesus talking to a Samaritan woman, not only were they amazed that he was spending time with such a woman, they were surprised that he was not really interested in the food they had brought him. His answer went totally over their heads: 'I have food of which you know nothing.' In other words, 'The diet I'm on is totally alien to you.' *'The disciples said to one another, "Has anyone brought Him anything to eat?" Jesus said to them, "My food is to do the will of Him who sent me, and to finish His work"' (Jn. 4:33-34).* You know why many are feeling unfulfilled and spiritually hungry? Simon has taken them out into the night where there is no food. The Peter in them is starving for the food of God's will, but Simon hates the diet. He has influenced them to eat the food of complacency, compromise and apathy. He has influenced you to eat the food of sensual soaps, gory gossip and fruitless retaliation. He has influenced you to eat the food of bad company, unnecessary work and a warm bed on Sunday morning. It's time to starve Simon and feed Peter. It's time to give Peter the food he craves: the food of God's will, God's Word and God's house.

Fifthly, Simon will influence you to remain spiritually immature.

John 21:7 tells us that John said to **Peter** *"'It is the Lord!" Now when Simon Peter heard . . .'* Every time the Word is preached or comes in rhema form from the Word, it is always directed to Peter – the Spirit man, the revelation-receiver. The Lord is directing revelation to Peter but Simon Peter hears it. The Lord is directing revelation to Peter, but Simon is still meditating on the latest gossip; he is still complaining about his recent or ancient hurt. He is still jealous over someone else's blessing, he is still pouting over an offence. When revelation comes to Peter in the form of a call, it's diluted because Simon says it's too hard. When revelation comes to Peter to go to a higher lever of discipleship, Simon says, 'Hold on to your old habits, I don't like change'. When revelation encourages Peter to pursue a deeper relationship with Jesus, Simon says, 'Don't go there, you'll turn into a religious freak.' Whatever you do, don't allow Simon to receive or interpret what God is giving to Peter: he will pollute it, dilute it and refute it until it's weak and insipid, causing you to stay spiritually immature and unable to mature and grow. *1 Corinthians 2:14* says, *'But the natural man (Simon) does not receive the things of the Spirit of God, for they are foolishness to him; nor can he know them, because they are spiritually discerned'* (brackets mine). What Paul is saying here is that when it comes to revelation, Simon is totally ignorant and incapable of understanding such things. Only Peter can grasp and apply spiritual things. Again, in *1 Corinthians 3:1-3*, while addressing the carnal church in Corinth, he says, *'And I, brethren, could not speak to you as to spiritual people but as to carnal, as to babes in*

Christ. I fed you with milk and not with solid food; for until now you were not able to receive it, and even now you are still not able; for you are still carnal,' i.e. influenced by Simon. When Jesus called out to the disciples from the shore, notice how he addressed them: *'Children, do you have any food?'* Yes, it was an affectionate appeal, but in the light of what we have just read, I believe it was a statement describing their immaturity.

Sixthly, Simon will influence you to meet Jesus covered.

John 21:7 says, *'Now when Simon Peter heard that it was the Lord, he put on his outer garment (for he had removed it) and plunged into the sea.'* How strange. Normally when you dive into the water you remove clothing, not put it on. I believe this is a perfect picture of what we sometimes do when preparing to meet Jesus. We come before him attempting to cover up something. It's totally futile, for 'All things are open and naked to the eyes of Him to whom we must give an account'. Any attempt we make to cover anything is as ridiculous as the leaves Adam and Eve used to cover their nakedness – pathetic and useless. Your covering must be removed before you can receive his covering. We become what Gordon MacDonald calls *'secret carriers'. David was a secret carrier. For a year he tried to live as if everything was business as usual, but his unrepentant past caught up with him. God had a wonderful future for David even though he had messed up, but before that destiny could be lived, he had to get David to realise that 'Whenever God becomes seriously involved as a rebuilder in your life, the issue of truth will be at the centre'.*

To move on in destiny, David realised he had to deal with truth. He shows us this lesson had been learned in his cry in *Psalm 51:6: 'Behold, You desire truth in the inward parts.'* Although Peter was prepared to meet Jesus with an outer garment, a mask, a covering, Jesus was about to face him with truth. Don't be a secret carrier before God. Don't meet him with an outer garment. The key to moving on in destiny is the dissolution of secrets and an embracing of truth. God asked Adam, compassionately, not, 'What have you done?' but, 'Where are you?' The incident of Simon Peter swimming to Jesus with an outer garment is, I believe, a perfect picture of the church. We desperately want a relationship with Jesus but are afraid to meet him naked for fear of judgement, so in fear of judgement and rejection we come before him in cosmetics.

God says, 'I've seen you without your make-up and I still love you.' He tenderly whispers to us, 'Wipe off the lipstick of unfulfilled promises and shallow, flattering praise. Tell me the truth with those lips. I'd rather have truth than lipstick. Wipe off the eye make-up of divided loyalty and misplaced attention: I love you without it. Just look me in the eye and give me your full attention without the eyeshadow and mascara. Wipe off the face powder of performance, penance and professionalism: you don't need it in my presence. Divine make-up has been provided by my love. Divine covering has been provided by my blood. Divine acceptance has been provided by my grace.'

The fact that we approach him with an outer covering, spiritual make-up and masks is simple proof that we still know very little about grace. *'Grace is released and accessed by simple honesty. Instead of fearing and denying all of my real or imagined shortcomings, I can embrace my humanity and see God pursuing me through it and in spite of it,'* writes Brennan Manning in *The Ragamuffin Gospel.* God appeals to us: **'Don't try to win my attention by wearing religious make-up, there is no need. I see you without it and love you the same.'**

Finally, Simon will influence you to live by law. In *John 21:10-11* Jesus says, *'"Bring some of the fish which you have just caught." Simon*

Peter went up and dragged the net to land, full of large fish, one hundred and fifty three.' Simon has to count; Simon can't handle grace; Simon is a legalist. Simon always has to search for a reason why God is blessing him. On one occasion he wanted Jesus to give him a mathematical formula for forgiveness. 'How many times must I forgive? Seven times? Forty-nine times? Give me a number, give me a rule.' But as Philip Yancey says in his wonderful book *What's So Amazing About Grace? 'God tears up the math of law and introduces another math – Grace.'* Law says two plus two equals four. An eye for an eye. Grace says the maths of grace doesn't add up. Simon Peter knew he didn't deserve such favour. He had failed and he was still living with the guilt of it; he deserved judgement and punishment, not grace. The Simon in us lives with a continual sense of guilt because he continually tries and continually fails to reach God's standard.

His favourite song is the anthem of the seven dwarfs. Instead of singing, 'Hi-ho, hi-ho, it's off to work I go,' he sings, 'I owe, I owe, so off to work I go. I fast and pray to earn my way because I owe.' To appease his guilt, Simon works more, prays more, reads more, overcompensates, because he fails to realise that grace doesn't count, grace doesn't add up.

Simon is more interested in image than in intimacy. Simon is the Pharisee's best friend – flesh trying to please God. Simon is more concerned with spiritual dermatology than with spiritual cardiology. Simon is more concerned with the avoidance of external contagion than with dealing with internal corruption. Simon passionately commits to dealing with the outside of the cup while failing to realise the cleanliness of the inside is more important. Simon's laws rule: don't touch, don't go, don't do. As long as he looks good on the outside, Simon believes he is doing OK. God has not called us to be avoiders of contagion but carriers of grace.

As I bring this final chapter to a close, I pray the realisation has hit you.

One of the key ingredients to David's success in defeating Goliath was his confidence in his own decisions. Refusing to play 'Simon says' with the devil will free the Peter in us to receive revelation and act out of a mature spiritual foundation, enabling us to make good decisions, finish our race, complete our destiny and be vessels God can use and prepare for greatness.

One Sunday morning I placed before my congregation a lump of dirty, unformed clay that had particles of stone, grass and other foreign objects sticking out of its sides. Next to this ugly, useless and unattractive lump I placed a beautiful vase, perfect in form and stunning in decoration. 'Use your imagination,' I told the people. 'The vase is shouting: how many want to be like me? The pile of clay was also shouting: how many want to be like me?' The answer is obvious, but how many Christians stay unformed, undeveloped, ugly and useless because they fight against the process of development in their lives? God says to us all, 'I'm never going to give you a life that makes me unnecessary. I'm never going to give you a dream, ask you to do something or take you through a process that leaves me unemployed in your life.' **If God becomes unnecessary in your life, where you are going is not where he is and what you're doing is something he's not in.**

For the shapeless lump of clay to become a useful vase of service, it has to submit to the process. My prayer is that this book will have opened your eyes to the truth or stirred you to remember that we are not born again into microwave Christianity. Preparation is essential for useful lives, and God is in the business of preparing us. In sharing something of my own experiences and understanding, I pray that you too, as you press towards your goal, will find joy in submitting to the process of allowing God to prepare you for greatness.

For a catalogue of Audio, Video and Printed Ministry of
Ray Bevan please contact

The Kings Church
69 Lower Dock Street, Newport, South Wales,
NP20 1EH UK

or visit our website @ www.kings-church.org.uk